A ROAD STRAIGHT AND TRUE

Isaiah 43:19-20

Living Bible (TLB)

[19] For I'm going to do a brand-new thing. See, I have already begun! Don't you see it? I will make a road through the wilderness of the world for my people to go home, and create rivers for them in the desert! [20] The wild animals in the fields will thank me, the jackals and ostriches too, for giving them water in the wilderness, yes, springs in the desert, so that my people, my chosen ones, can be refreshed.

Ten Days to Total Financial Freedom

Ten Days of Discovery Searching the Hidden Treasures of the Deep

By Marvin Swanson

Ten Days to Total Financial Freedom

Title: Ten Days to Total Financial Freedom
Subtitle: Ten Days of Discovery Searching the
Hidden Treasures of the Deep
Author: Marvin Swanson

ISBN: 9780992104603

NOTE: The Voice Translation of the Bible used in
various places has _**italicised**_ commentary
included in the text.

The Dedication Page

I could make a list a mile long thanking many different people who have been an inspiration to me as well as giving correction, instruction, and encouragement all through my life. But most of all I want to thank God for a praying grandmother who never gave up on me in spite of my opposition to her faith and her God when I was a youth.

I know there were others who prayed for me as well, including my parents. But God showed me plainly that it was my Grandmother Sitler's prayers that He answered for my salvation in 1981, sixteen years after my grandmother had passed away and went home to Jesus, and her heavenly reward.

The Holy Spirit broke this stubborn heart of mine when He showed me this and I wept for days. Me, the one who had ridiculed grandma, persecuted her, taunted her, and mocked her at every opportunity … it still makes me weep … I'm weeping now. May God have mercy on me and may all of her prayers be answered. May I no more be a discredit to her, or my family name, either this earthly one, or my new family of believers in Jesus. May God, who is faithful, see to it that every one of Grandma's prayers is answered, all these many years later.

Thank God for the faithfulness of a praying family and the faithfulness of a God and Savior who refuses to allow even one prayer to fall to the ground unanswered. Grandma never saw the answer to her fervent intercession for me in this life, but in the life to come, YES! YES! YES!

This is a book of dedication and thankfulness to the faithfulness of a praying Grandmother who never gave up on this wayward son. Consistently at 8 pm every evening, after the farm chores and supper were finished, she would go to her upstairs room in our old farmhouse and sing hymns from her Mennonite Hymn book and pray ... for me ... her own sons and daughters and their spouses ... all eight x 2 of them ... and her many grandchildren ... some like me, who did not understand our praying Grandma and thought she was too "religious and outdated."

Grandmother often said to me, with a scolding finger, "If the Good Lord would have meant for you to smoke, He would have given you a chimney." She also told me to "seek the Lord while He may be found, call upon Him while He is near" (Isaiah 55:6) and gave me my first Bible in 1957, when I was ten. Faithfulness! The very character of God (Psalm 89:8, 27-39.) Thank's most of all to a covenant keeping God who never fails to make good on His promise!

Marvin.

THE FAITHFULNESS OF GOD

Isaiah 55:10 (TLB) As the rain and snow come down from heaven and stay upon the ground to water the earth, and cause the grain to grow and to produce seed for the farmer and bread for the hungry, **11** so also is my word. I send it out, and it always produces fruit. It shall accomplish all I want it to and prosper everywhere I send it. **12** You will live in joy and peace. The mountains and hills, the trees of the field—all the world around you—will rejoice. **13** Where once were thorns, fir trees will grow; where briars grew, the myrtle trees will sprout up. This miracle will make the Lord's name very great and be an everlasting sign of God's power and love.[a]

Table of Contents

Introduction

This book is a message about financial freedom beginning with a right relationship with our Creator God who has never been in debt or financial difficulty but understands both perfectly.

This book is about order and coming back to the Father in heaven through faith in Jesus, the Son of God, who was tempted in every way, yet without sin. Jesus became qualified to be our Champion and the Captain of our Salvation in every area of life through the things He suffered. As a result He is become our merciful and faithful High Priest before God, a Priest who would be both merciful to us and faithful to God in dealing with the sins of the people. For since he himself has now been through suffering and temptation, he knows what it is like when we suffer and are tempted, and he is wonderfully able to help us. Hebrews 2 (Paraphrase).

This book is about mentorship and leadership from the One and Only who is truly qualified to fulfill this role.

This book is about rulership and submission to the King of the Universe, who created the mountains and the hills, the sun, moon, and stars and everything between.

Ten Days to Total Financial Freedom

This book is about Him who owns the cattle on a thousand hills, created the silver and gold and hidden treasures of the deep, fills the oceans with teeming life, calls forth the wind and weather, and waters the earth with ease.

This book is about the Lord of the harvest, the God who never fails on His promise.

This book is about a love relationship as the firm foundation from which true financial freedom stems. For Jesus said, "What shall it profit a man if he gain the whole world, but loses his soul?"

This book is about coming back to the true source of all wisdom, understanding, knowledge, wealth, and power. For without Him (Christ) nothing would exist, For by him were all things created, that are in heaven, and that are in the earth, visible and invisible, whether they be thrones, or dominions, or principalities, or powers: all things were created by him and for him: And he is before all things, and by him all things consist. Colossians 1:16-17 KJV. Jesus is the supreme mentor of this universe and perfectly qualified at every level in every area of life, including our finances.

This book is about loving God first and foremost and secondly about prospering under his leadership and being supremely fruitful in his service in the kingdom of God on earth. It is a book about Mary (devotion) at the feet of Jesus, before Martha (action) serving at His table.

This book is about mentorship at the highest level. It is about obedience to the Word of God and submission to the guidance and direction of the Holy Spirit. It is about knowing the heart of the Father in heaven and serving Him for his glory and our benefit and that of many others.

It is a book about Kingdom increase and my part in his great harvest. My part begins at the foot of the cross of Jesus Christ and continues in my surrendered life, abiding in the Vine, my attitude of servanthood being "not my will but your will be done" and my position of sonship as an heir of God and joint-heir with Jesus Christ. *For I have not received the spirit of bondage again to fear; but I have received the Spirit of adoption, whereby I cry, Abba, Father.* Roman 8: 15

This book is about coming back to our roots, the beginning, the source; coming back to a place of absolute trust and confidence in the God of mercy, grace, and truth. The One who truly loves us and seeks our good because He is love and He is good. Recognizing He is 100% faithful to his character and consistent in His dealings with us, His creation.

Ten Days to Total Financial Freedom

God is God and God is good. There is no other. He has chosen to reveal Himself through the person of His Son, Jesus Christ. This is the firm foundation of our faith and trust and this is the fountain from which we draw our strength. God is love and those who love dwell in God and He in them. This is our well spring and from this fountain of life we prosper and share our abundance with others for the purpose of revealing Jesus, the Lamb of God, and the expansion of God's eternal Kingdom in the earth. This is our mission and God's purpose for our increase.

Enjoy!

Your friend,

Marvin Swanson.

1. In The Beginning

In the beginning God created the heaven and the earth. Genesis 1:1

"In the beginning" sounds like a great place to start any project. In this case our project is discovering God's will for my prosperity. In the beginning the earth was a shapeless, chaotic mass, with the Spirit of God brooding over the dark vapors. Shapeless? Chaotic? This sounds like financial messes in the 21st century.

When finances are out of control and debt and expenses are more than the income this is the picture. Chaotic is a polite word and dark vapors describe angry creditors with threatening letters and phone calls. The good news is God has a plan.

The Holy Spirit is still hovering over the vapors of my life and waiting God's command, "Let there be light:" ... and there was light ... When God speaks things happen, things change. In the beginning God brought order into the universe when He divided the light from the darkness and called the light Day and the darkness He called Night. And the evening and the morning were the first day. God had a plan and He spoke this plan into existence through the power of His Word. This plan was to bring forth order into His universe. God still has a plan. It has not changed. It is a plan of salvation and bringing things back into order in my own life. This includes my finances.

Divine order. This is the order of the Universe. God is a God of order. He ordered the heavens and the earth into being and that which was chaotic, unruly, and in disarray followed His instructions and came into line with His will. God's plan for His creation has not changed in spite of man's fall from grace in the garden of Eden, Genesis 3. His plan is to bring order into the chaotic mess I refer to as "my life here on earth."

And where did this mess begin? It began in the garden with the original sin of disobedience and rebellion against the instructions of God. Instead of Divine order now chaos, death, destruction, sickness, and poverty began its reign of terror in the earth; unruly, lawless; out of control. Disorder became the rule of the day. Disconnect from God became the ruler of the night. The distinction between light and darkness, good and evil became blurred and the order God had established in the beginning fell back into its former state, shapeless and chaotic. A world filled with sin and rebellion no longer recognizing the boundaries set by a loving Creator God. The world was a mess once again only now it was a created mess having some sense of shape and form but fallen from God's grace.

This is where it all began through the sin of one man, Adam, all of us have been born into this world with his fallen nature. An injury happened at the fall and the result is the continuing effects as evidenced by a world filled with chaos, crime, rebellion, disarray, disharmony, out of joint with its Creator and one with another, sickness, disease, poverty, lack, want, death and destruction on every side regardless of nationality, skin color, or culture. This is the bad news.

The good news is by one man, Jesus Christ, many are made righteous, brought back into right relationship with the Father in heaven and Divine order being re-established. Light and darkness once again become separate and distinct. The lines between right and wrong, good and evil, no longer blurred. As we draw closer to our Loving God through faith in His Son, once again we begin to enjoy the benefits of His presence and His provision the first Adam lost. Through the first Adam all have sinned and come short of the glory of God. Through the Second Adam, Jesus Christ, many are made right. God's order re-established (Romans 5:19). Amen!

Ten Days to Total Financial Freedom

God had a plan. God has a plan. It's a plan for my life. A plan for good not evil. It's a plan for my increase and prosperity to give me a hope and a future under the guidance of His Spirit and in accordance with His will. Jeremiah 29:11.

Step # 1: In this view what is my definition of financial freedom? My definition may differ from yours so the question remains, what is YOUR definition? Make a list of your present needs and further break it down to how much for each expenditure. What is your income? Do they match, or do the expenses exceed the income?

Next, tithes, charitable giving, etc. Is your definition of financial freedom having enough to cover all these areas or are you looking for increase in your giving and your ability to provide for your home and family?

Write out YOUR definition. Invite the Holy Spirit to help you. He was there in the beginning of creation and He will be there for you in your re-creation.

Remember, this is step #1 in bringing order back into your financial world. In effect you are saying, "Let there be light:" ... and the first rays of sunshine will begin to shine on the mess, beginning to make distinction, giving it shape and form.

2. Total Separation

What fellowship does light have with darkness?

2 Corinthians 6:14-18

Easy-to-Read Version (ERV)

We Are God's Temple

14 You are not the same as those who don't believe. So don't join yourselves to them. Good and evil don't belong together. Light and darkness cannot share the same room. 15 How can there be any unity between Christ and the devil[a]? What does a believer have in common with an unbeliever? 16 God's temple[b] cannot have anything to do with idols, and we are the temple of the living God. As God said,

"I will live with them

and walk with them;

I will be their God,

and they will be my people."

17 "So come away from those people

and separate yourselves from them, says the Lord.

Don't touch anything that is not clean,

and I will accept you."

18 "I will be your father,

and you will be my sons and daughters,

says the Lord All-Powerful."

Footnotes:

2 Corinthians 6:15 the devil Literally, " beliar," one form of the Hebrew word " belial," which means "worthlessness" and was used to refer to the devil or the enemy of Christ.

2 Corinthians 6:16 God's temple God's house— the place where God's people worship him. Here, it means that believers are the spiritual temple where God lives.

Easy-to-Read Version (ERV)

Copyright © 2006 by World Bible Translation Center

Separation from the works of darkness are a basic requirement for fellowship and friendship with God. The question is, "do I want friendship with God, who is Light? Or do I still crave friendship with the world, which is still in chaos and darkness? Which do I desire more? God's presence and His provision? Or the world's consolations and comforts which appeal to my sinful nature? Which is more important to me, money and the riches of this world and all it promises? Or friendship with God and all He promises? This is the choice I must make and it is from this point I begin my journey into true financial freedom with God, or further into the chaotic darkness of serving the false god, Mammon/Money.

God is a jealous God and having any other gods in our lives is a violation of the first commandment. Exodus 20:1-6. Jealous in the sense that it is He who created us in the first place and it is He who has made a way for us to be delivered from the bondage of sin, death, hell, and destruction. Jealous in the same sense a loving parent is concerning their own children.

It is well for us to remember that it is God who has power over life and death, not money or any other earthly commodity. One day I will stand before the judgment seat of Jesus Christ, not the judgment seat of Money. I will give an account to Him and to Him alone for my words and my works in this earth realm. Turning from any known idols in my life brings me once again into the light of His mercy and grace. Once again Divine order is established and peace is the result. Peace with God. Peace with myself. Peace in my finances. Righteousness, peace, and joy have come to my house (Romans 14:17). HalleluJAH!

Step # 2: What does God's word say about money? Knowing the truth will set me free to follow Him with confidence and full assurance of faith, aware that God loves me and cares for me as His very own son or daughter. How valuable is this? What is this knowledge of God and my relationship with Him worth in terms of dollars and cents? Does it have value that can be expressed in these earthly terms? His eye is on the sparrow and I know He watches over me. Is this knowledge worth a million dollars in the bank? What if the economy changes and my million becomes pennies? What then? What if my "sure fire" investment sours and goes bad? Then what? Where is my faith? Where is my trust? Where is my confidence placed for the future? Money sometimes lies, but God never does. Money and earthly wealth offer great promise, but does not always deliver, and in fact, without God in the equation cannot bring prolonged satisfaction. On the other hand, God offers great promises and never fails to make good, for every promise of God is "yes" and "amen" in Jesus Christ.

This is the dilemma. Is it true then, that money is evil? I have heard this quoted many times. Communists believe that "money is the root of evil." Is this true? Is this what the Bible declares? Believe it or not the Bible has more to say about money than almost any other subject, and in fact, it was God who came up with the idea in the first place. Armed with this information should help us understand that money is definitely NOT the root of all evil as some have suggested, but rather, the LOVE OF MONEY is the root of all evil, as Paul tells us, 1 Timothy 6:10. Simply put, the LOVE OF MONEY is a form of COVETEOUSNESS WHICH IS IDOLATRY (Colossians 3:5). It is an idol in the temple of God and Jehovah God will not allow any other gods before Him!

Money is mentioned many times in the Bible, well over 100 times, in the King James Version. This does not include words like gold and silver, or other riches, or inheritances, or other related topics, including poverty. The Bible talks about money more than almost any other topic.

Gold and silver, were simply two forms of currency used during Bible times. Once again, in the King James Version, gold is mentioned more than 400 times and silver more than 300.

Financial matters are mentioned more often in the Bible than prayer, or the many miracles, or even God's mercy. Only sin is mentioned more.

The fact that money in and of itself is not evil is clear in God's Word, however we are to guard ourselves against the love of money and attachment to it.

Hebrews 13:5 says, "Keep your lives free from the love of money and learn to be content with what you have, because God has said, 'Never will I leave you.'"

In Matthew 6:24, Jesus says, "No one can serve two masters. Either he will hate the one and love the other, or he will be devoted to the one and despise the other. You cannot serve both God and money."

1 Timothy 6:10 states, "For the love of money is a root of all kinds of evil. Some people, eager for money, have wandered from the faith and pierced themselves with many griefs."

As we will see in a later chapter one of the Biblical antidotes for covetousness is the tithe and caring for the poor and needy.

In view of the above information I must see money as neither evil nor good. It is simply an earthly commodity provided by the Lord as an exchange for goods or services between persons. The evil is the desires lurking in our own hearts. Money, or the lack thereof, simply reveals the location of our heart towards God. Is money where I have placed my trust or is it firmly planted in the Lord and His promised provision? Money can be used for either good or evil. It can be used to buy a gun to rob a bank or it can be used to open an account for deposit from the proceeds of honest labor. You decide. Is money good? Or evil? Communists claim money is the root of evil and as a result hate capitalists, yet they do not hesitate to kill or deal in illicit trade to get their hands on more and more of this neutral commodity.

Ephesians 4:28

The Voice (VOICE)

28 If you have been stealing, stop. Thieves must go to work like everyone else and work honestly with their hands so that they can share with anyone who has a need.

Great instructions from the Holy Spirit through His anointed servant, Paul the Apostle. This is the Biblical concept and general attitude towards work and money. It's a good thing and it's a sure step towards God's order and separation of light and darkness.

For all those who have adopted an anti-Biblical, socialistic, welfare, "the world owes me" mentality, take heed to these words from God's Holy Word. This is the will of God according to the Word of God and this is God's order of doing business. God's blessing rests upon all those who honor His Word through their submission to it and corresponding actions of obedience. But God's wrath remains upon all who take His instructions lightly, thinking they can prosper and increase apart from the light of His Word.

Remember, God spoke the world into existence through the power of His spoken Word, and God has the ability to breathe life back into my chaotic world through my simple cooperation according to His written Word.

Total Separation from everything and anything that in any way distracts, distorts, or diminishes my definition of "10 Days To Total Financial Freedom."

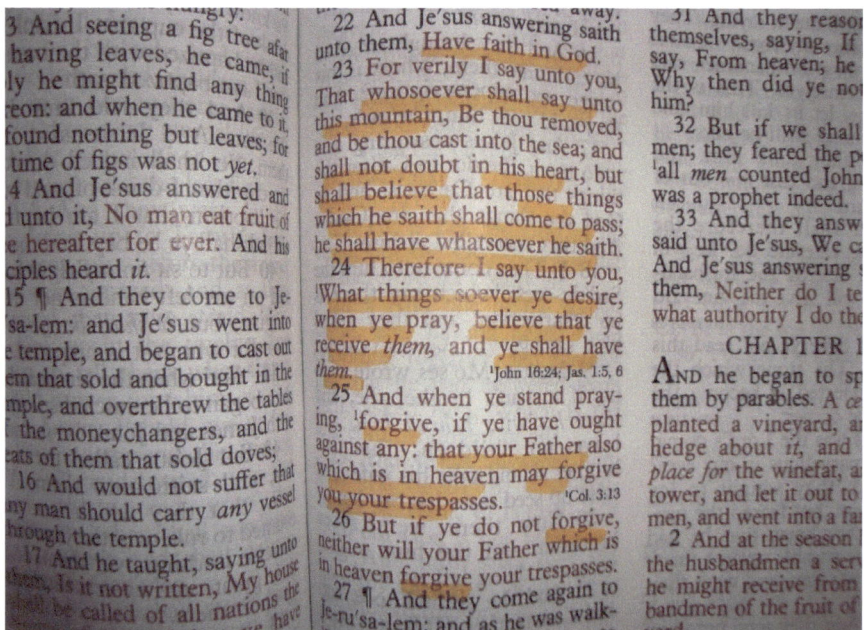

Faith in God Conquers Fear

3. Face Your Fears

Name them ... one by one and call them exactly what they are.

1 Samuel 17:1-11

Contemporary English Version (CEV)

Goliath Challenges Israel's Army

17 The Philistines got ready for war and brought their troops together to attack the town of Socoh in Judah. They set up camp at Ephes-Dammim, between Socoh and Azekah.[a] 2-3 King Saul and the Israelite army set up camp on a hill overlooking Elah Valley, and they got ready to fight the Philistine army that was on a hill on the other side of the valley.

4 The Philistine army had a hero named Goliath who was from the town of Gath and was over nine feet[b] tall. 5-6 He wore a bronze helmet and had bronze armor to protect his chest and legs. The chest armor alone weighed about one hundred twenty-five pounds. He carried a bronze sword strapped on his back, 7 and his spear was so big that the iron spearhead alone weighed more than fifteen pounds. A soldier always walked in front of Goliath to carry his shield.

8 Goliath went out and shouted to the army of Israel:

Why are you lining up for battle? I'm the best soldier in our army, and all of you are in Saul's army. Choose your best soldier to come out and fight me! 9 If he can kill me, our people will be your slaves. But if I kill him, your people will be our slaves. 10 Here and now I challenge Israel's whole army! Choose someone to fight me!

11 Saul and his men heard what Goliath said, but they were so frightened of Goliath that they couldn't do a thing.

Footnotes:

17.1 Socoh and Azekah: Socoh was controlled by the Israelites, while Azekah was in Philistine hands.

17.4 over nine feet: The Standard Hebrew Text; the Dead Sea Scrolls and some manuscripts of one ancient translation have "almost seven feet."

The above story from the Bible is a great illustration of the power of fear ... v11, Saul and his men were so frightened they couldn't do anything. This is what fear does; fear paralyzes us and renders us useless and limits our production. The Israelite army was in a state of confusion and immobilized by one single giant which they feared more than anything. What are the fears in my life? Am I facing giant problems that look as big as this? The problem Saul and his army were facing had a name and a face. He could be easily identified and discerned. Have I taken the time to properly identify and discern the enemies I fear and have me paralyzed? What is crippling me and impeding my forward progress? What is standing in the way of me getting that promotion or better income I need to maintain my "definition of total financial freedom?" For surely I have an enemy. Serving God means I have a natural enemy no different than the Philistines being the natural enemies of Israel. In my case, Satan, is my sworn enemy. He is the enemy of God and he is naturally the enemy of anyone wanting to serve God. God's enemy is my enemy. Satan has not changed his tactics. He still works through the realm of intimidation and fear. So the questions remain:

- What is intimidating me?
- What fear is keeping me from moving forward towards my definition of total financial freedom?
- What is holding me back?
- What makes me tremble in fear at the thought of attempting?
- What causes anxiety when I think about it?

The answer to these questions will reveal my real enemy and my real fear.

Saul's army had no problem identifying their real enemy. He was big, strong, proud, loud mouthed, and strutted himself back and forth in front of them for 40 days, shouting obscenities at them and mocking them and their God. This is Satan's primary tactic, producing fear which paralyzes through intimidation. He attempts to demoralize and conquer through this show of superiority, but it's all a pretense. Like the shepherd boy, David, who faced this giant and conquered him with only a sling and a stone through faith in the name of the Lord of hosts (1 Samuel 17:40-47), so Jesus conquered over the devil on the cross 2000 years ago and stripped him of his swagger and defiance against the Living God and God's people ...

Colossians 2:11-15

The Voice (VOICE)

11 In Him you were also circumcised, set apart by a spiritual act performed without hands. The Anointed One's circumcision cut you off from the sinfulness of your flesh. 12 You were buried with Him beneath the waters of the ceremonial washing called baptism[a] and then were raised up with Him by faith in the resurrection power of God, who brought Him back from the dead. 13 And when your flesh was still uncircumcised— dead in transgression and swathed in its sinful

nature; it was God who brought us[b] to life with Him, forgave all our sins, and 14 eliminated the massive debt we incurred by the law that stood against us. He took it all away; He nailed it to the cross. But that's not all. 15 He disarmed those who once ruled over us—those who had overpowered us. Like captives of war, He put them on display to the world to show His victory over them by means of the cross.

Amen! And Amen!!! This is the greatest news ever! Jesus is our "David" and Satan our "Goliath." As surely as the young shepherd, David, defeated the "fear" of Israel, our Good Shepherd, Jesus Christ, has defeated our greatest fear on the cross. He has wiped away the fear of God's judgment because of our sin by nailing all the charges against us to His cross and marking the debt we owed, "PAID IN FULL!"

He further stripped Satan of all his power to intimidate us through the fear of death, hell, and the grave, by triumphing over them for us through His death, burial, and resurrection!!! (1 Corinthians 15:51-58).

We no longer fear loss because we know in whom we believe and we have confidence of our future because of Him who holds our future in His hands! Our trust is in Him, not in things, persons, or possessions.

This is our confidence and this is our armor. David used a sling and a stone and faith in the Lord of hosts. We use the promise of God and through faith in the God of the promise we conquer our fears, for THE BATTLE IS THE LORD'S, 1 Samuel 17:47.

What is my greatest fear? Name it! Confront it! Satan's only weapon is intimidation through fear. All he can do is taunt. Take the Sword of the Spirit which is the Word of God and slay this toothless imposter who goes about as a roaring lion seeking someone to devour! Jesus pulled the giant's teeth on Calvary 2000 years ago. His roar is worse than his bite. Face the enemy head on and as smoke is driven by the wind, God's promise spoken from your lips and acted upon in faith will drive this "vapor" far from you. As wax melts before the flame, so shall this fraud melt away from the flame of God's Word pouring from you. (Note: Psalm 68:1-4).

Behold, the fear of the Lord, that is wisdom; and to depart from evil is understanding. (Job 28:28). We fear God and His Word, not the evil giants who come against us. Amen!

4. Rebuild on a Sure Foundation of Faith and Love

Perfect love casts out fear, 1 John 4:18, and we overcome the world by our faith, 1 John 5:4.

All that counts with God is faith which works (motivated) by love, Galatians, 5:6.

Abraham was counted as righteous and called the Friend of God because he believed God, mixing his obedience with his faith, James 2:21-23. Abraham's love for God was proven when God asked for his son of promise, Isaac, on the altar of sacrifice. Abraham's heart was proven in this when he placed Isaac upon the altar ready to slay him as an act of worship unto the Lord. What was more important to Abraham? His relationship with the Lord who had given him this son of promise? Or was the son of promise more important than the God who had promised? The gift? Or the Giver of the gift? Abraham chose the Giver of life over the gift and God provided a substitute for his son. A ram caught in a thicket by its horns and Abraham named this place Jehovah-Jireh, the Lord will provide. This was a demonstration of Abraham's faith which was motivated by his supreme love for his God and Provider. Abraham's heart had been proven. No idols there. His worship and service to his Lord and King was pure and holy. Abraham's faith and life were firmly established upon a solid foundation. Abraham could be trusted with the riches of this world simply because they did not possess him. He possessed them.

Thus God could say to Abraham … Genesis 22

The Voice

Special Messenger: Abraham! Abraham!

Abraham: I am right here!

Special Messenger: 12 Don't lay your hand on the boy or do anything to harm him. I know now that you respect the one True God and will be loyal to Him and follow His commands, because you were willing to give up your son, your only son, to Me.

13 Abraham glanced up and saw a ram behind him with its horns caught in the thicket. He went over, dislodged the ram, and offered it up as a burnt offering in the place of his son. 14 From that day forward, Abraham called that place, "The Eternal One will provide." Because of this, people still today say, "On the Mount of the Eternal, all will be provided."

15 The special messenger of the Eternal One called out to Abraham yet a second time from heaven.

Special Messenger: 16 Listen to the solemn vow the Eternal One has spoken: "Because you have done what I asked and were willing to give up your son, your only son, 17 I will reaffirm My covenant of blessing to you and your family.[a] I will make sure your descendants are as many as the stars of the heavens and the grains of sand on the shores. I reaffirm My earlier promises that your descendants will possess the lands and sit in the gates of their enemies, 18 and from your descendants all the peoples of the earth will discover true blessing.[b] **All this is because you have obeyed My voice.**

We reach the climax of Abraham's covenant story. God tests Abraham, and he passes with flying colors. Somehow he knows God will provide, for he tells his servants that he and his son will come back from the mountain. He also knows that God's covenant promises are going to be fulfilled through Isaac and not another. Although Abraham is willing to sacrifice him, he expects Isaac to still be the one through whom God's blessings come to the world. How could it all happen? Only God knows, and Abraham trusts in God and His promises. Abraham's level of trust is unmatched in all of Scripture. This is why he stands as the founding father of our faith.

End of Bible quote.

At the top of Abraham's **"People I Love"** - **"Things I Love" - Places I Love"** list, would be GOD in all three categories. By his actions he proved that God was in first place above his love for Isaac. His response to God's call to worship proved this was the thing he loved more than any other. It was top priority. Abraham loved to be in the place of God's presence proven by his obedience to go to the mountain God had designated for their meeting. **GOD was the Person, the Thing, and the Place, Abraham honored most of all,** thus he was called the Friend of God and trusted with the riches of God for the purpose of expanding God's kingdom and influence in the earth.

What's on my list of "People - Things - Places?" What are my priorities? Is God at the top of my list in each category? Have I made a list? Have I measured myself in this mirror? How many blemishes do I see? Hopefully not many. Hopefully God is at the top and the idols of pride, ambition, self-exaltation, self-seeking and the riches of this world have taken their rightful place at the feet of Jesus near the cross.

Ten Days to Total Financial Freedom

If I make a list and compare that to a list Jesus would make, how would it look? Somehow I think the people, things, and places, Jesus would prioritize may look somewhat different than mine. For example when I think of people I love I think of people I know, family, friends, etc. When I think of things I love, I might include new computer, office chairs, paintings, posters, coffee at Juan Valdez or OMA, etc. etc. When I think of places I love, I immediately think of places I've been in different parts of the world, Ukraine, South America, China, etc. My List contains mainly things that can be classified as earthly.

Now how would Jesus' list look?

People Jesus Loves: the humble, the meek, the merciful, the poor in spirit, the persecuted for His names sake, the broken hearted, those with a contrite heart, the repentant, the faithful, the righteous who trust Him by faith, the pure in heart, the charitable, the obedient, to name a few.

Things Jesus Loves: Kindness, forgiveness, reconciliation, goodness, mercy, faith, hope, charity, truthfulness, grace, courtesy, humility, etc.

Places Jesus Loves: Resting in the promises of God, contentment, abiding, caring, sharing, loving one another, peace, joy, abundance, satisfaction, prayer, worship, the Garden of Gethsemane was such a place, for Jesus and His disciples often came here for times of rest, relaxation, restoration, healing, further instruction, prayer, worship, interaction with God and with one another, John 18:1-2. Together these are some of the People, Things, and Places Jesus loved and still loves today.

How does this list differ from mine? His list is much more spiritual in the sense of being directed more towards the soul and the inner man. My list is much more earthy or human, in the sense of being more outer directed towards my five senses. The things on my list might not be evil in and of themselves and in fact be valuable and have their place, but the inner qualities of the heart, not the outer which perishes, should be my priority. This is a great way to check my heart and see where the foundation of my faith and believing really is. If I love Jesus, then the people, things, places, He loves I should love also.

Remember, faith in the Person and the promises of God motivated by the love of God is my only sure foundation. I'm rebuilding on a better footing. The light of the gospel of God's grace is beginning to penetrate the deep darkness of my soul and restore right order to my life. No more idols of the heart. No more darkness concerning who God is and what His will is for me. The chaotic, shapeless mess that marked my life is now beginning to take form and make some sense. To God be the glory for great things He is doing in me!

Luke 4:18-19 New Living Translation (NLT)

[18] "The Spirit of the LORD is upon me,
for he has anointed me to bring Good News to the poor.
He has sent me to proclaim that captives will be released,
that the blind will see,
that the oppressed will be set free,
[19] and that the time of the LORD's favor has come.[a]"

5. Time is a Seed

Someone said, "time is money." If this is true and time is of the essence and time is money, then where, what, how, and when should I be investing time to MAXIMIZE my results?

What does God value? What do I value? God is bringing order into my life so by now my values should be coming more into line with His values. How did Jesus view His time spent on earth?

John 9:1-7

Contemporary English Version (CEV)

Jesus Heals a Man Born Blind

9 As Jesus walked along, he saw a man who had been blind since birth. 2 Jesus' disciples asked, "Teacher, why was this man born blind? Was it because he or his parents sinned?"

3 "No, it wasn't!" Jesus answered. "But because of his blindness, you will see God work a miracle for him. 4 As long as it is day, we must do what the one who sent me wants me to do. When night comes, no one can work. 5 While I am in the world, I am the light for the world."

6 After Jesus said this, he spit on the ground. He made some mud and smeared it on the man's eyes. 7 Then he said, "Go and wash off the mud in Siloam Pool." The man went and washed in

Siloam, which means "One Who Is Sent." When he had washed off the mud, he could see.

John 4:27-38

Contemporary English Version (CEV)

27 The disciples returned about this time and were surprised to find Jesus talking with a woman. But none of them asked him what he wanted or why he was talking with her.

28 The woman left her water jar and ran back into town. She said to the people, 29 "Come and see a man who told me everything I have ever done! Could he be the Messiah?" 30 Everyone in town went out to see Jesus.

31 While this was happening, Jesus' disciples were saying to him, "Teacher, please eat something."

32 But Jesus told them, "I have food that you don't know anything about."

33 His disciples started asking each other, "Has someone brought him something to eat?"

34 Jesus said: My food is to do what God wants! He is the one who sent me, and I must finish the work that he gave me to do. 35 You may say that there are still four months until harvest time. But I tell you to look, and you will see that the fields are ripe and ready to harvest. 36 Even now

the harvest workers are receiving their reward by gathering a harvest that brings eternal life. Then everyone who planted the seed and everyone who harvests the crop will celebrate together. 37 So the saying proves true, "Some plant the seed, and others harvest the crop." 38 I am sending you to harvest crops in fields where others have done all the hard work.

Jesus was not a time waster. Even as a youth twelve years old, Jesus was found in the temple in the midst of the learned men both listening and asking questions. And all that heard him were astonished at his understanding and answers. Jesus said to his parents, "do you not know that I must be about my Father's business?" Luke 2:46-49.

Jesus was on a mission. He had an assignment from the Father. Jesus never allowed Himself to deviate from this calling. He knew His Father in heaven. He knew His plan of salvation for the world. He knew the character and the heart of His Father. He knew who He was, the Son of God, come to the earth for one holy purpose. To reveal the nature of the Father, full of grace and truth. And to redeem fallen man from the curse of the law and a lost eternity by the blood of His own sacrifice on the cross as God's spotless Passover Lamb.

This was His mission; His assignment; His calling. He was the Light of the world and God's order was being re-established on a personal level through the born again experience, through faith in the blood of His sacrifice on the cross, thus ending Satan's chaotic reign of terror, death, and destruction in the life of the believer. Satan, who had usurped and stolen the first Adam's kingdom authority through lies and deception in the Garden of God, was judged and soundly defeated at the cross of Christ. The final execution of this judgment will come at the end of the thousand year rule and reign of Christ on the earth according to Revelation 20, when Satan and his followers will be thrown into the burning lake of fire. Then the new earth, new heaven, and new Jerusalem and a home with Jesus, the Lamb of God, the Father, and the saints of all time, forever free from sin and darkness, Revelation 21-22. Amen! And Amen!

For this purpose the Son of God was manifested, that He might destroy the works the devil had done, 1 John 4:8

In the beginning God said, "Let there be light:" and there was light. A great separation took place between light and darkness. The one He called Day, the other He called Night. Now the very One who was the Light of the world and in fact the One who had created the light in the first place had come into a fallen world of great darkness, chaos, confusion, mistrust, evil, sickness, disease, poverty, brokenness, lack, and want. And as you would expect the Light began to right the wrong and bring God's order back into an unruly, tumultuous world, still under the rule of the Prince of Darkness; the Prince of this world, Satan, which he had wrested from the hands of the first Adam through deceit.

Now comes on the scene the One the Bible refers to as the Second Adam or the Last Adam, Jesus Christ (1 Corinthians 15:45), and the natural order of things at His appearance begins as you would expect. The Light casts out the darkness and overthrows Satan's kingdom in the same way a bright light chases away the dark night. Let there be Light: and there was light. This is the plain and simple, long and short of it all. In the beginning of creation God said and it was so.

Now in this time of new beginning, Jesus, the Son of God, conceived of the Holy Spirit in the womb of a virgin, born the Son of Man, has arrived; God's Redeemer for a fallen race and a fallen world. God's order was being re-established, re-introduced, and restored through the Light of the world. Through faith in Christ Jesus my Lord and Savior I am a new creation and part of this new order.

2 Corinthians 5:17-21

Easy-to-Read Version (ERV)

17 When anyone is in Christ, it is a whole new world.[a] The old things are gone; suddenly, everything is new! 18 All this is from God. Through Christ, God made peace between himself and us. And God gave us the work of bringing people into peace with him. 19 I mean that God was in Christ, making peace between the world and himself. In Christ, God did not hold people guilty for their sins. And he gave us this message of peace to tell people. 20 So we have been sent to speak for Christ. It is like God is calling to people through us. We speak for Christ when we beg you to be at peace with God. 21 Christ had no sin, but God made him become sin[b] so that in Christ we could be right with God.

Footnotes: 2 Corinthians 5:17 When anyone … world Or "Anyone who is in Christ is a new creation." 2 Corinthians 5:21 sin Or "an offering for sin."

This is the New World Order. Anything or anyone that claims to be part of a new world order apart from this revelation of Jesus Christ contained in the Word of God, is deceived and blinded by the god of this fallen world, the Prince of the power of the air, Ephesians 2:1-3. The same liar who deceived the first man and woman in the beginning is still at work. His tactics of deception have not changed. He still offers the forbidden fruit from the tree of the knowledge of good and evil with the same false promise, Genesis 3:4 (ERV) But the snake said to the woman, "You will not die. 5 God knows that if you eat the fruit from that tree you will learn about good and evil, and then you will be like God!"

A visit to the morgue and a tour past the local cemetery should be all the proof necessary to convince anyone who is still in doubt about the validity of God's Word and the deception and lies of the evil serpent called Satan, the Devil, the Snake, the Deceiver.

Jesus, who is the Truth, conquered over Satan, who is the Liar. Whose side are you on? Who are you serving? What are you believing? Do you know who you are? A child of God through faith in the Son? Or a child of darkness still believing a lie? Who are you? Have you discovered God's will for your life? If not, why not? Do you know your high and holy calling in Christ Jesus, your Lord and Savior? If not, why not? Do you know your God given assignment and Divine ordination, John 15:16? If not, why not? What's your problem? Now is the time to spend your time wisely, seeking the King of Glory with all your heart, mind, soul, and strength until you find Him.

Jeremiah 29:10-14

New Living Translation (NLT)

10 This is what the Lord says: "You will be in Babylon for seventy years. But then I will come and do for you all the good things I have promised, and I will bring you home again. 11 For I know the plans I have for you," says the Lord. "They are plans for good and not for disaster, to give you a future and a hope. 12 In those days when you pray, I will listen. 13 If you look for me wholeheartedly, you will find me. 14 I will be found by you," says the Lord. "I will end your captivity and restore your fortunes. I will gather you out of the nations where I sent you and will bring you home again to your own land."

This was God's Word to the ancient Israelites who were being held captive in Babylon and this Word is still true for you and I today. It's all about God's restoration and new world of order according to His plans, not mine. God has a plan and He will see the plan through to the logical conclusion. This plan of God includes me. Do I know His plan for my life? Have I sought Him whole heartedly until His will, His calling, His assignment for my life has become crystal clear?

Jesus had no doubts about who He was or what His assignment was and neither should I. Go for it Christian Soldier! Seek the Lord until He be found!

Isaiah 50:4-10

New Living Translation (NLT)

The Lord's Obedient Servant

4 The Sovereign Lord has given me his words of wisdom, so that I know how to comfort the weary. Morning by morning he wakens me and opens my understanding to his will.

5 The Sovereign Lord has spoken to me, and I have listened. I have not rebelled or turned away.

6 I offered my back to those who beat me and my cheeks to those who pulled out my beard. I did not hide my face from mockery and spitting.

7 Because the Sovereign Lord helps me, I will not be disgraced. Therefore, I have set my face like a stone, determined to do his will. And I know that I will not be put to shame.

8 He who gives me justice is near. Who will dare to bring charges against me now? Where are my accusers? Let them appear!

9 See, the Sovereign Lord is on my side! Who will declare me guilty? All my enemies will be

destroyed like old clothes that have been eaten by moths!

10 Who among you fears the Lord and obeys his servant? If you are walking in darkness, without a ray of light, trust in the Lord and rely on your God.

Jesus was on assignment. He determined in His heart to fulfill His Father's will. He set His face as a stone and refused to deviate from the plan of God. He conquered over the temptations of the devil in the wilderness with "IT IS WRITTEN" and so can we.

Jesus spent all of His time in the center of His heavenly Father's will, researching, studying, praying, worshipping, speaking, and doing. Note: John 5:19-20.

How am I spending mine? Am I investing my time in trivial pursuits or in persons, things, and places that count for both time and eternity? God knows and He will help me with my understanding in these things.

For everything there is a time and a season under the sun. Let's not neglect the most important time we spend seeking the Lord in this season of doing His will and completing our assignment as laid out by the Master Planner and Designer of this universe.

Time is my seed to the future. How I spend my time determines my rewards both now in this life and in the life to come. May God help me number my days and spend my time wisely, for His glory, my benefit, the benefit of many others, and the expansion of His eternal kingdom.

If "time is money" how am I doing with this commodity portioned to me in equal 24 hour installments each day? How am I doing with my definition of financial freedom?

6. Lifestyle

What was Jesus lifestyle?

It's a good idea to study the life of someone who was never in debt, never had an unpaid bill, was never late on a mortgage or rent payment, always had more than enough for his own needs and lots to give away to the needy, had the ability to feed thousands with crumbs until they were satisfied and full with baskets left over, paid his taxes on time in full, and needed a treasurer in his company.

Does this sound like me? If not, why not? Could I be studying wrong role models? Could I have allowed the concepts and instructions of this fallen world system to be my mentors? Could it be that the age old Serpent, the Liar, the Deceiver, Satan, has dominated my financial world through his misinformation and outright lies? Has darkness, chaos, debt, and destruction been my financial portion? If so it's time to turn on the lights! It's time to change my focus; time to change my lifestyle.

Jesus life was more about lifestyle than about destination. Jesus taught by His Words and by His Works. His works were the miracles He performed in His heavenly Father's name. His miracles were a testimony of who He was. They confirmed His words. The Words and the Works of Jesus Christ bring forth life, peace, joy, healing, deliverance, salvation, reconciliation. Jesus lived a lifestyle of peace, joy, obedience, humility and absolute surrender to the will of His Father in Heaven.

The result? Everywhere Jesus went darkness was conquered by the Light. The deaf heard. The dumb talked. The lame walked. The lepers were healed. The sick restored to health and well-being. The hungry were fed. The dead were raised to life.

This is exactly what you would expect from someone who claimed to be the Son of God, the Light of the world, The Living Bread of God come down from heaven, The Living Water who gives eternal drink. Emmanuel, God with us. And you shall call his name, Jesus, Savior.

Jesus lifestyle was one of Divine order and ordination. When the angel of the Lord spoke to the virgin Mary and said that she would conceive in her womb and bring forth a son and call his name Jesus, in effect this messenger sent by God was saying, **"Let there be Light."** Note: Luke 2:26-38. **And at His birth there was Light.** Read Luke 2:1-40.

This is God's pattern for restoration, reshaping, and remaking, and this applies to my finances as surely as it applies to my eternal soul. God speaks His Word into my dark world of debt, financial struggle and turmoil. In effect this Word from God is His "Let there be light" to me personally. It is God's personal address to my unique problem. It is God's order. God's command. Be healed. Be made whole. God saying, be made in My image. Be restored. Come in to My Light and My freedom. Come to me. Adopt My lifestyle of quiet submission to the Father's will. Humbly submit to My plan for your life. Trust in the Master's Plan with full assurance of faith and confident trust that My Plan is much better than yours; my Plans for your success in this life and in the next.

Isaiah 30:15

New Living Translation (NLT)

15 This is what the Sovereign Lord, the Holy One of Israel, says: "Only in returning to me and resting in me will you be saved. In quietness and confidence is your strength. But you would have none of it.

God invites His people to lean only on Him. If they will just stop their busyness and self-reliance, God will be able to take care of them.

But you refused.

Blessings for the Lord's People

18 So the Lord must wait for you to come to him so he can show you his love and compassion. For the Lord is a faithful God. Blessed are those who wait for his help.

Jesus was the Ultimate Sower

A. A life marked by humble submission and explicit obedience to the Father's will.

B. A life marked by compassion, love, mercy, truth, giving, caring, sharing.

C. A life marked by self-sacrifice

D. A life marked by prayer and devotion to His Father in Heaven

E. A life marked by willingness to serve

F. A life marked by sowing - everywhere Jesus went He sowed seeds of truth, love, mercy, forgiveness, kindness, grace, compassion, reconciliation, and ultimately His life sown as a seed through His death on the cross; His love a seed sown for us while we were yet in sin and His enemies. What kind of love is this? What kind of Sower would perform such an act of mercy and compassion as this? What kind of Mentor is this? Is this the lifestyle of a Champion? Is this the lifestyle that leads to abundance? Is this the answer to my financial mess?

Remember, Jesus never owed a dime to anyone, always paid His bills on time, fed multitudes with crumbs, needed a treasurer, and helped the poor. He never lacked for a place to sleep although He owned no real estate. His Father in Heaven was His security and His provision for the vision. Jesus never lacked a day in His entire life. Even during His 40 day fast in the wilderness where He was tempted of the devil, He was supplied with all the strength He needed to carry Him through and at the end Angels ministered to Him. There was always enough and more than enough in His life. Jesus was surrounded by the miracles and provisions of God and never lacked any good thing from the hand of His Heavenly Father. Isn't this what financial freedom is about? Financial freedom is more about seeking after God and adopting the lifestyle of the Supreme Commander in Chief of the Lord's Army, Jesus Christ. Financial freedom is more about this than about seeking earthly wealth and possessions that will soon perish with the using. This latter is the mentorship offered according to the dictates of this fallen world.

"Let there be Light."

7. Code of Conduct

The Kingdom Rule of Thumb

2 Timothy 2:15

New Living Translation (NLT)

An Approved Worker

15 Work hard so you can present yourself to God and receive his approval. Be a good worker, one who does not need to be ashamed and who correctly explains the word of truth.

God has an established order or standard for doing Kingdom business no different than this world system has an order. We live in an ordered universe even though the world has been grossly distorted and perverted by sin. However, there are some things that will never change.

Notice the sun, moon, and stars. The sun always comes up in the east and goes down in the west. The sun never fails. The sun is 100% consistent in its place. There are 24 hours in each and every day and that never fails. The earth rotates on its axis without fail and never misses a single day. The earth orbits the sun every 365 1/4 days without fail. People are born. People live a prescribed length of time on the earth. People die. It never fails. There is an order to everything. The sun rises. The sun sets. The four seasons follow one another in order; seedtime and harvest, cold and heat, night and day. One follows the other.

Every skilled tradesman knows there is a code of conduct unique to their profession; an electrical code for the Electrician, a plumbing and heating code for the Plumber, a building code for the Architect, Engineer and building trades. Each has its own standard and code of conduct.

The Kingdom order is God first, me second; always and without variation. God's way, not my way if my way is contrary to His. All Kingdom rule starts with God first. This is the Light we need to navigate our way through this darkened world of sin and confusion. We are discussing finances and financial freedom from God's perspective. I won't exhaust everything the Word of God says about this but give enough to whet the appetite and give solid direction. The rest will be up to the reader to pursue further.

Malachi 3:6-12

Easy-to-Read Version (ERV)

Stealing From God

6 "I am the Lord, and I don't change. You are Jacob's children, and you have not been completely destroyed. 7 But you never obeyed my laws. Even your ancestors stopped following

me. Come back to me, and I will come back to you." This is what the Lord All-Powerful said. "You say, 'How can we come back?'

8 "People should not steal things from God, but you stole things from me. "You say, 'What did we steal from you?' "You should have given me one-tenth of your things. You should have given me special gifts. 9 In this way your whole nation has stolen things from me, so bad things are happening to you."

10 The Lord All-Powerful says, "Try this test. Bring one-tenth of your things to me. Put them in the treasury. Bring food to my house. Test me! If you do these things, I will surely bless you. Good things will come to you like rain falling from the sky. You will have more than enough of everything. 11 I will not let pests destroy your crops. All your grapevines will produce grapes." This is what the Lord All-Powerful said.

12 "People from other nations will be good to you. You will have a wonderful country." This is what the Lord All-Powerful said.

This is one of the most powerful scriptures in the Bible and the only place where God challenges us to "PUT HIM TO THE TEST!" It's all about money and giving to the work of God through tithes and offerings. Some of the most amazing promises in the Bible concerning our finances are here in these few verses. Promises of God's supernatural abundance and supernatural protection. Promises of favor with other people and other nations.

Our part in this? Follow His code of conduct through obedience to the tithe. This almost sounds too good to be true, but then again, why not try the Word of God and put God to the test as He challenges the disobedient. What if this doesn't work? Then God would be a liar and His word not true.

On the other hand what if this does work? When was the last time I seen God's financial blessing falling on me like rain from heaven? What do I have to lose? Let's see ... what's 10% of not enough to pay my bills and stay on top of my finances? According to this quick calculation I can see that I really have nothing to lose, I'm already losing, but I have everything to gain if God's promise proves true.

There are many scriptures throughout the Bible concerning tithes and giving, beginning with Abram paying tithes to Melchizedek, King of Salem, Genesis 14:18-20.

Isaac sowed in a time of drought and famine according to God's command and received a 100 fold return on his investment, Genesis 26:1-14.

Jacob promised a tithe to the Lord in response to God's help and protection upon his life, Genesis 28:20-22.

The God of Abraham, Isaac, and Jacob has not changed. He is the same, yesterday, today, and forever, Hebrews 13:8. He is my God. In Him who never changes will I place my trust. Amen.

2 Corinthians 9:6-15

The Voice (VOICE)

Giving away money is one of the hardest things believers do, especially when there are bills to pay and more expenses than income. However, helping others with their physical needs and not only their spiritual needs is a fundamental principle of Christian spirituality. Perhaps it would be easier to give our financial resources if we could turn away from our own continual consumption and live simpler lifestyles. Then there would be not only the willingness but also the ability to share God's blessings with others.

6 But I will say this to encourage your generosity: the one who plants little harvests little, and the one who plants plenty harvests plenty. 7 Giving grows out of the heart— otherwise, you've reluctantly grumbled "yes" because you felt you had to or because you couldn't say "no," but this isn't the way God

wants it. For we know that "God loves a cheerful giver."[a] 8 God is ready to overwhelm you with more blessings than you could ever imagine so that you'll always be taken care of in every way and you'll have more than enough to share. 9 Remember what is written about the One who trusts in the Lord: He scattered abroad; He gave freely to the poor; His righteousness endures throughout the ages.[b] 10 The same One who has put seed into the hands of the sower and brought bread to fill our stomachs will provide and multiply the resources you invest and produce an abundant harvest from your righteous actions. 11 You will be made rich in everything so that your generosity will spill over in every direction. Through us your generosity is at work inspiring praise and thanksgiving to God. 12 For this mission will do more than bring food and water to fellow believers in need—it will overflow in a cascade of praises and thanksgivings for our God. 13 When this mission reaches Jerusalem and meets with the approval of God's people there, they will give glory to God because your confession of the gospel of the Anointed One led to obedient action and your generous sharing with them and with all exhibited your sincere concern. 14 Because of the extraordinary grace of God at work in you, they will pray for you and long for you. 15 Praise

God for this incredible, unbelievable, indescribable gift!

Footnotes: 9:7 Proverbs 22:8 … 9:9 Psalm 112:9

Once again we read words that are almost incredible for us to believe. Are these words really in the Bible? I thought God wanted me sick, poor, destitute, and broke, so He could teach me better? According to these words God cannot want me in this condition. I must have been hearing and believing the devil and his lies. Then again I must remember, in the beginning God brought order and structure into the world when He spoke it all into being and said "Let there be light: and there was light." Is it possible that these are words of light and grace and truth that God has sent to me to get me started on my path to recovery to TOTAL FINANCIAL FREEDOM?

Surely.

Proverbs 10:4

The Voice (VOICE)

4 A slack hand produces nothing but poverty, but an industrious hand soon takes hold of riches.

What did Jesus say about giving and work ethics?

Matthew 23:23

New Living Translation (NLT)

23 "What sorrow awaits you teachers of religious law and you Pharisees. Hypocrites! For you are careful to tithe even the tiniest income from your herb gardens,[a] but you ignore the more important aspects of the law—justice, mercy, and faith. **You should tithe, yes, but do not neglect the more important things.**

Footnotes:

23:23 Greek tithe the mint, the dill, and the cumin.

Luke 21:1-4

New Living Translation (NLT)

The Widow's Offering

21 While Jesus was in the Temple, he watched the rich people dropping their gifts in the collection box. 2 Then a poor widow came by and dropped in two small coins.[a] 3 "I tell you the truth," Jesus said, "this poor widow has given more than all the rest of them. 4 For they have given a tiny part of their surplus, but she, poor as she is, has given everything she has."

John 12:1-8

The Voice (VOICE) Jesus Anointed at Bethany

12 Six days before the Passover feast, Jesus journeyed to the village of Bethany, to the home of Lazarus who had recently been raised from the dead, 2 where they hosted Him for dinner. Martha was busy serving as the hostess, Lazarus reclined at the table with Him, 3 and Mary took a pound of fine ointment, pure nard (which is both rare and expensive), and anointed Jesus' feet with it; and then she wiped them with her hair. As the pleasant fragrance of this extravagant ointment filled the entire house, 4 Judas Iscariot, one of His disciples (who was plotting to betray Jesus), began to speak.

Judas Iscariot: 5 How could she pour out this vast amount of fine oil? Why didn't she sell it? It is worth nearly a year's wages;[a] the money could have been given to the poor.

6 This had nothing to do with Judas's desire to help the poor. The truth is he served as the treasurer, and he helped himself to the money from the common pot at every opportunity.

Jesus: 7 Leave her alone. She has observed this custom in anticipation of the day of My burial. 8 The poor are ever present, but I will be leaving.

Footnotes:

12:5 Literally, 300 denarii, Roman coins

What did Jesus think about tithes, offerings, and giving? He thought this was great and still does. Remember? He's the same yesterday, today, and forever. He never changes. This is why we can trust Him explicitly and take His word to heart. Every promise of God is "yes" and "amen" complete in Him. (2 Corinthians 1:20). Sacrificial giving is close to the heart of God and still leaves a sweet fragrance wherever it's poured out.

Giving is an established fact and rule of conduct in God's Kingdom and carries with it great promises of increase and multiplication. The Lord Jesus Himself being the Ultimate Sower, sowed His own life on Calvary and 2000 years later the harvest of souls is still coming in.

John 12:24-25

The Voice (VOICE)

24 I tell you the truth: unless a grain of wheat is planted in the ground and dies, it remains a solitary seed. But when it is planted, it produces in death a great harvest. 25 The one who loves this life will lose it, and the one who despises this life in this world will have life forevermore.

This is The Law of the Harvest and a Kingdom Principle that never grows old or wears out. Jesus was this grain of wheat planted in the ground and He says to us, "follow Me." This is the starting place, the beginning ground, the foundation and platform of a great future harvest of increase and multiplication.

The Words and the Works of Jesus Christ.

Jesus, the Ultimate Sower, sowed His love and His life into everyone who came to Him, and by His selfless lifestyle of sowing, began the restoration of God's Kingdom order and Code of Conduct in the lives of all those He touched. If "time was money" then Jesus spent much of His ministering and caring for the poor. Jesus was never too busy to stop by the roadside for one of these.

8. Order in Our Work

Everything must ultimately come into order and be subject to the discipline and authority of the Holy Spirit and the Word of God. If we are to enjoy God's blessings of abundance and increase then it follows that we must adhere to His plan of action, His blueprint, His roadmap to success, His instructions.

Luke 5:1-11

The Voice (VOICE)

5 Picture these events:

On the banks of Gennesaret Lake, a huge crowd, Jesus in the center of it, presses in to hear His message from God. 2 Off to the side, fishermen are washing their nets, leaving their boats unattended on the shore.

3 Jesus gets into one of the boats and asks its owner, Simon, to push off and anchor a short distance from the beach. Jesus sits down and teaches the people standing on the beach.

4 After speaking for a while, Jesus speaks to Simon.

Jesus: Move out into deeper water, and drop your nets to see what you'll catch.

Simon (perplexed): 5 Master, we've been fishing all night, and we haven't caught even a minnow. But . . . all right, I'll do it if You say so.

6 Simon then gets his fellow fishermen to help him let down their nets, and to their surprise, the water is bubbling with thrashing fish—a huge school. The strands of their nets start snapping under the weight of the catch, 7 so the crew shouts to the other boat to come out and give them a hand. They start scooping fish out of the nets and into their boats, and before long, their boats are so full of fish they almost sink!

The miracles Jesus performs come in all types: He heals the sick. He frees the oppressed. He shows His power over nature. He will even raise the dead. But as the story in verses 21-26 shows, one of the greatest miracles of all is forgiveness. To have sins forgiven—to start over again, to have God separate believers from their mistakes and moral failures, to lift the weight of shame and guilt—this may well be the weightiest evidence that God's Son is on the move. The kingdom of God doesn't throw all guilty people in jail; God doesn't execute everyone who has made mistakes or tell them they're just getting what they deserve. Instead, it brings forgiveness, reconciliation, a new start, a second chance. In this way, it mobilizes believers to have a new future. Certainly Jesus has communicated the message of the Kingdom through words and through signs and wonders. Now Jesus embodies the message in the way He treats people, including outcasts like Levi. As a tax collector, Levi is a Jew who works for the Romans, the oppressors, the enemies. No wonder tax collectors are despised! But how does Jesus treat this compromiser? He doesn't leave him paralyzed in his compromised position; He invites him—like the paralyzed man—to get up and walk, and to walk in a new direction toward a new King and Kingdom.

8-10 Simon's fishing partners, James and John (two of Zebedee's sons), along with the rest of the fishermen, see this incredible haul of fish. They're all stunned, especially Simon. He comes close to Jesus and kneels in front of His knees.

Simon: I can't take this, Lord. I'm a sinful man. You shouldn't be around the likes of me.

Jesus: Don't be afraid, Simon. From now on, I'll ask you to bring Me people instead of fish.

11 The fishermen haul their fish-heavy boats to land, and they leave everything to follow Jesus.

The Words and the Works of Jesus Christ. This is the Kingdom order of doing business with God. Our words without corresponding works/actions, are dead and useless according to James 2:14-26. Our works confirm and solidify our faith making this real and powerful, life changing and tangible. Our works confirm and prove our doctrine is true and from the Lord. Our right actions help authenticate our words.

John 5:36-38

New Living Translation (NLT)

36 But I have a greater witness than John—my teachings and my miracles. The Father gave me these works to accomplish, and they prove that he sent me. 37 And the Father who sent me has testified about me himself. You have never heard his voice or seen him face to face, 38 and you do not have his message in your hearts, because you do not believe me—the one he sent to you.

Luke 19:13

The Voice (VOICE)

13 Before his departure, he called 10 of his servants and gave them each about three months of wages.[a] "Use this money to buy and sell until I return."

Jesus encourages industry and honest employment with a view towards increase and multiplication. In our story from Luke 5 we see that His disciples have been on the lake fishing all night and catching nothing. Discouraged they are on the shore washing their nets when Jesus comes by and asks Peter if He can use his boat as a preaching platform to reach the growing crowds of people. Peter complies and pushes the boat a little way from shore.

When Jesus is done speaking to the people he says to Peter and the others, " Move out into deeper water, and drop your nets to see what you'll catch." At first Peter responds reluctantly, but then he decides to obey the Voice of the One he is learning to trust and he and the others push out into deeper water as Jesus said.

This was their first act of self-denial. Their will in submission to His. The seed of their wills being sown into the soil of His promise, to "see what you will catch." This was done in accordance to the will of the One who is the Light of the world and the Lord of Life.

Prepare for a miracle harvest, for this act of submission is **a burial ground.** This is the place where the seed falls into the ground and dies. Next they drop their nets as instructed. They are following the instructions of the One who created order in the beginning and who created the sea and the fish they contain. If anyone in the universe knows where the "catch" is it's Him!

This letting down of their nets according to His word is a symbol of their surrender. It is the place where they discover the true power of unconditional surrender to the Voice of their

Lord and Savior. It is the place of the **"White Flag."** It is marked by death to self but alive unto God their Savior. They are surrendering to a much Higher Power than they.

They are about to get the shock of their lives when their nets and their boats are so full of the fish they couldn't find on their own fishing all night, that these seasoned veterans of the sea can hardly believe their eyes. It is a true miracle from the Lord of the sea, who speaks and the winds and waves obey His every instruction. The fish of the deep obey His voice. The dead leap to their feet at His command. The blind beggars see. The deaf hear. The dumb talk. The lame walk. Shouldn't we pay more attention to this One who walks on water and quiets all our fears too?

And what does this miracle of abundance produce in Peter and the others?

8-10 Simon's fishing partners, James and John (two of Zebedee's sons), along with the rest of the fishermen, see this incredible haul of fish. *They're all stunned, especially Simon.* **He comes close to Jesus and kneels in front of His knees.**

Simon: I can't take this, Lord. I'm a sinful man. You shouldn't be around the likes of me.

This was Simon Peter's response ... **one of humility and a feeling of complete unworthiness at the greatness of His Lord, Savior, and Master.**

Where did all of this take place?; at the place of obedience and trust; at the place of coming into Divine Order. The place of agreement with the spoken Word of God. The place of burial; the place where Peter's will fell as a seed into the rich soil of "God's will be done." It was the two becoming one. The marriage of the seed and the soil, here at the place of the "White Flag." Marriage with the Lamb of God will always produce an abundant harvest, for Jesus has come to give us life and that more abundantly. John 10:10.

John 15:1-17 He is the Vine and Giver of life, I am the branch.

The Voice (VOICE)

15 Jesus: I am the true vine, and My Father is the keeper of the vineyard. 2 My Father examines every branch in Me and cuts away those who do not bear fruit. He leaves those bearing fruit and carefully prunes them so that they will bear more fruit; 3 already you are clean because you have heard My voice. 4 Abide in Me, and I will abide in you. A branch cannot bear fruit if disconnected from the vine, and neither

will you if you are not connected to Me. 5 I am the vine, and you are the branches. If you abide in Me and I in you, you will bear great fruit. Without Me, you will accomplish nothing. 6 If anyone does not abide in Me, he is like a branch that is tossed out and shrivels up and is later gathered to be tossed into the fire to burn. 7 If you abide in Me and My voice abides in you, anything you ask will come to pass for you. 8 Your abundant growth and your faithfulness as My followers will bring glory to the Father.

At a time when all of His disciples are feeling as if they are about to be uprooted, Jesus sketches a picture of this new life as a flourishing vineyard— a labyrinth of vines and strong branches steeped in rich soil, abundant grapes hanging from their vines ripening in the sun. Jesus sculpts a new garden of Eden in their imaginations—one that is bustling with fruit, sustenance, and satisfying aromas. This is the Kingdom life. This is all about connection, sustenance, and beauty. But within this promise of life is the warning that people must be in Christ or they will not experience these blessings.

Jesus: 9 I have loved you as the Father has loved Me. Abide in My love. 10 Follow My example in obeying the Father's commandments and receiving His love. If you obey My commandments, you will stay in My love. 11 I want you to know the delight I experience, to find ultimate satisfaction, which is why I am telling you all of this.

12 My commandment to you is this: love others as I have loved you. 13 There is no greater way to love than to give your life for your friends. 14 You celebrate our friendship if you obey this command. 15 I don't call you servants any longer; servants don't know what the master is doing, but I have told you everything the Father has said to Me. I call you friends. 16 You did not choose Me. I chose you, and I orchestrated all of this so that you would be sent out and bear great and perpetual fruit. As you do this, anything you ask the Father in My name will be done. 17 This is My command to you: love one another.

Whatever our work. Whatever our calling or vocation we should do all things with all our might, with excellence, as unto the Lord.

Colossians 3:22-25

New Living Translation (NLT)

22 Slaves, obey your earthly masters in everything you do. Try to please them all the time, not just when they are watching you. Serve them sincerely because of your reverent fear of the Lord. 23 Work willingly at whatever you do,

as though you were working for the Lord rather than for people. 24 Remember that the Lord will give you an inheritance as your reward, and that the Master you are serving is Christ.[a] 25 But if you do what is wrong, you will be paid back for the wrong you have done. For God has no favorites.

And a word for the employer…

Colossians 4:1

The Voice (VOICE)

4 And to you masters: treat your slaves fairly and do what is right, knowing that you, too, have a Master in heaven.

Remember the fisherman? Remember the great miracle harvest? It is the Lord we are serving and obeying when we do our work with excellence and it is the Lord Himself who commands our increase. Drop our nets of pride and stubborn wills and let them become intertwined with His in humility and submission. Let the seed fall into the ground and marry the soil. Let the rich soil of obedience to His will produce an abundant, overflowing harvest. And may this increase result in greater giving to the work of the ministry and the saving of many more souls. May this marriage of wills open the way for promotion and increase on my road to Total Financial Freedom. It's all for the glory of God and the increase of His Kingdom. The sun in the eastern sky is beginning to rise on my finances and the darkness of debt, lack, and want, is beginning to fade. I have hope for a better day coming as my words and works begin to come into order and match with His. Amen!

Philippians 4:19 New Living Translation (NLT)[19] And this same God who takes care of me will supply all your needs from his glorious riches, which have been given to us in Christ Jesus. (Where God guides, He provides. God's work done God's way, will never lack for God's supply.)

9. Goals - Our Primary Focus

Matthew 6:19-34

The Voice (VOICE)

19 Some people store up treasures in their homes here on earth. This is a shortsighted practice—don't undertake it. Moths and rust will eat up any treasure you may store here. Thieves may break into your homes and steal your precious trinkets. 20 Instead, put up your treasures in heaven where moths do not attack, where rust does not corrode, and where thieves are barred at the door. 21 For where your treasure is, there your heart will be also.

22 The eye is the lamp of the body. You draw light into your body through your eyes, and light shines out to the world through your eyes. So if your eye is well and shows you what is true, then your whole body will be filled with light. 23 But if your eye is clouded or evil, then your body will be filled with evil and dark clouds. And the darkness that takes over the body of a child of God who has gone astray—that is the deepest, darkest darkness there is.

When Jesus speaks of eyes and light, He means all people should keep their eyes on God because the eyes are the windows to the soul. Eyes should not focus on trash—pornography, filth, or expensive things. And this is what He means when He says, "Where your treasure is, there your heart will be also."

Jesus: 24 No one can serve two masters. If you try, you will wind up loving the first master and hating the second, or vice versa. People try to serve both God and money—but you can't. You must choose one or the other.

25 Here is the bottom line: do not worry about your life. Don't worry about what you will eat or what you will drink. Don't worry about how you clothe your body. Living is about more than merely eating, and the body is about more than dressing up. 26 Look at the birds in the sky. They do not store food for winter. They don't plant gardens. They do not sow or reap—and yet, they are always fed because your heavenly Father feeds them. And you are even more precious to Him than a beautiful bird. If He looks after them, of course He will look after you. 27 Worrying does not do any good; who here can claim to add even an hour to his life by worrying?

28 Nor should you worry about clothes. Consider the lilies of the field and how they grow. They do not work or weave or sew, and yet their garments

are stunning. 29 Even King Solomon, dressed in his most regal garb, was not as lovely as these lilies. 30 And think about grassy fields—the grasses are here now, but they will be dead by winter. And yet God adorns them so radiantly. How much more will He clothe you, you of little faith, you who have no trust?

31 So do not consume yourselves with questions: What will we eat? What will we drink? What will we wear? 32 Outsiders make themselves frantic over such questions; they don't realize that your heavenly Father knows exactly what you need. **33 Seek first the kingdom of God and His righteousness, and then all these things will be given to you too.** 34 So do not worry about tomorrow. Let tomorrow worry about itself. Living faithfully is a large enough task for today.

Jesus had a goal ... to complete the assignment given Him by His father in Heaven ...

John 17:1-5

The Voice (VOICE)

17 Jesus (lifting His face to the heavens): Father, My time has come. Glorify Your Son, and I will bring You great glory 2-3 because You have given Me total authority over humanity. I have come bearing the plentiful gifts of God; and all who receive Me will experience everlasting life, a new

intimate relationship with You (the one True God) and Jesus the Anointed (the One You have sent). 4 **I have glorified You on earth and fulfilled <u>the mission</u> You set before Me.** 5 In this moment, Father, fuse Our collective glory and bring Us together as We were before creation existed.

Paul had a goal ... centered on Christ

Philippians 3:7-15

The Voice (VOICE)

7 But whatever I used to count as my greatest accomplishments, I've written them off as a loss because of the Anointed One. 8 And more so, I now realize that all I gained and thought was important was nothing but yesterday's garbage compared to knowing the Anointed Jesus my Lord. For Him I have thrown everything aside— it's nothing but a pile of waste—so that I may gain Him. 9 When it counts, I want to be found belonging to Him, not clinging to my own righteousness based on law, but actively relying on the faithfulness of the Anointed One. This is true righteousness, supplied by God, acquired by faith. 10 I want to know Him inside and out. I want to experience the power of His resurrection and join in His suffering, shaped by His death, 11 so that I may arrive safely at the resurrection from the dead.

The crucified and risen Jesus is the model that Paul desires to embody by walking deep in His pathway of death and life—suffering and resurrection.

12 I'm not there yet, nor have I become perfect; but I am charging on to gain anything and everything the Anointed One, Jesus, has in store for me—and nothing will stand in my way because He has grabbed me and won't let me go. 13 Brothers and sisters, as I said, I know I have not arrived; **but there's one thing I am doing: I'm leaving my old life behind, putting everything on the line for this mission**. 14 **I am sprinting toward the only goal that counts: to cross the line, to win the prize, and to hear God's call to resurrection life found exclusively in Jesus the Anointed.** 15 All of us who are mature ought to think the same way about these matters. If you have a different attitude, then God will reveal this to you as well.

I have a goal ... a new one

My goal is to achieve Financial Freedom in 10 Days. This is now day 40 in my serious quest to accomplish it. But the further I come and the more I seek God's will and the deeper I go into His word the more I discover that total financial freedom is not as much about money as about relationship. It's more about my relationship to

God and to money than about bank accounts or size of income. God knows we need both and has already made this provision ahead of time, Matthew 6:32. God knows we need money for survival and for service, but this should not be our main focus. This is a secondary issue.

By now it is becoming abundantly clear that God's provision is more about relationship and lifestyle than about numbers or quantities. True financial freedom is not determined by the size of my bank account. True financial freedom is resting in the knowledge that God loves me and that His provision will always be sufficient and abundant. This is the nature of God. The Lord is not a hoarder. He is a giver. No good thing will He withhold from those who walk uprightly according to His will and trusting in Him.

Psalm 84:10-12

King James Version (KJV)

10 For a day in thy courts is better than a thousand. I had rather be a doorkeeper in the house of my God, than to dwell in the tents of wickedness.

11 For the Lord God is a sun and shield: the Lord will give grace and glory: no good thing will he withhold from them that walk uprightly.

12 O Lord of hosts, blessed is the man that trusteth in thee.

With all of this in view then what should be my financial goal? With the Lord as my sun and shield shouldn't this be security enough? My new goal should be more about coming into line with God's Word and His will for my life than about money. My new goal should be more about getting to know Him and His ways more and more. It should be more about increasing my level of faith and trust in the One and only true source of everything I will ever need to be successful in this life.

My goal should read more like "**10 Days To Total Trust In the Lord My Provider.**" This would be more in line with the Words of Jesus in Matthew 6. This would be more like the apostle Paul's goal which he recommends to all who are mature enough to receive it, Philippians 3:15.

Paul's goal sounds more like Jesus' goal in John 17.

My goal, like my list of people I love, things I love, places I love, is a little off compared to Jesus list of people, things, and places. It should come as no surprise that my financial goal and main pursuit in life is also I little askew from the mark. If I want to hit the bulls-eye with God I need to refocus on the things that are most important to Him. This is what it means to take His yoke and the definition of discipleship which is what Jesus commanded ...

Matthew 28:18-20

Voice

Jesus: I am here speaking with all the authority of God, who has commanded Me to give you this commission: 19 **Go out and make disciples in all the nations.** Ceremonially wash them through baptism in the name of the triune God: Father, Son, and Holy Spirit. 20 **Then disciple them. Form them in the practices and postures that I have taught you, and show them how to follow the commands I have laid down for you.** And I will be with you, day after day, to the end of the age.

Wow! Wow! Wow! What else can I say to this? This is the Light of the world speaking with the authority of heaven. In effect He is saying, "Let there be light" in no uncertain terms. **This is God's New World Order!** It is patterned after the Risen Savior, Jesus Christ. The Second Adam who accomplished what the first Adam failed to do. Namely, live fully submitted to the will and word of his Heavenly Father. This is the heavenly pattern the first Adam discounted and chose his own will over that of his Lord and Maker.

Jesus conquered over sin, hell, death, and the grave through His willful submission and obedience to the Father's will. By His obedience Jesus was perfectly yoked to the Father in life and in death and in His resurrection. Death and the devil could not hold Him down. The grave could not restrain Him. On the third day He arose just as He had prophesied to His disciples before He went to the cross as the sacrificial Lamb of God for our sin.

Jesus goal is my goal. Paul's goal is my goal. My goal has shifted somewhat. My "people, things, and places" list has also changed. I am coming more into line with the Light of the world, who also called Himself the Way, the Truth, and the Life, and that no man could come to the Father except through Him.

Jesus is the Way

Jesus is the Truth

Jesus is the Life

Jesus is the Light

Jesus is the Door

Jesus is the Savior

Jesus is the Healer

Jesus is the Deliverer

Jesus is my Provider

I have a new goal ... **"10 Days of Discovery In Knowing Jesus More and More Better and Better Deeper and Deeper"**

Remember Jesus words to the fisherman? "Push out a little deeper and see what you will catch." Dig a little deeper into God's Word. Go a little deeper into your relationship with the Master of the sea. Deepen your knowledge of Him and His will for your life. Deeper in love with the One who is Love. Deeper, deeper still. The miraculous catch is in the deeper water, the deeper relationship. The harvest of plenty is there deep in the bosom of the Father. The secrets to your success are hidden there deep in the heart of God ...

1 Corinthians 2:9-10

The Voice (VOICE)

9 But as the Scriptures say, No eye has ever seen and no ear has ever heard and it has never occurred to the human heart All the things God prepared for those who love Him.[a] 10 God has shown us these profound and startling realities through His Spirit. The Spirit searches all things, **even the deep mysteries of God.**

Footnotes:

2:9 Isaiah 64:4

My goal? **"10 More Days Discovering The Heart Of God With The Help Of The Holy Spirit"**

If part of God's plan is to make me a millionaire so I can further extend His kingdom through my increased financial giving, then so be it. The revelation of this mystery will be revealed to me by the Holy Spirit as, by faith, I row out into the deeper water of God's holy Word and begin to plumb the depths of God's heart with my renewed nets of confidence and trust. Trusting in His love, mercy, grace, and truth to show me the way. In this way I will "catch" all the provision I will ever need, whether it be of a spiritual or a physical nature. Praise God forever! HalleluJAH!

In reviewing my goals I must revisit the scripture I began this discourse with ...

Genesis 1:1-5

The Voice (VOICE)

1 In the beginning, God created everything: the heavens above and the earth below. Here's what happened: 2 At first the earth lacked shape and was totally empty, and a dark fog draped over the deep while God's spirit-wind hovered over the surface of the empty waters. Then there was the voice of God.

God: 3 Let there be light.

And light flashed into being. 4 God saw that the light was beautiful and good, and He separated the light from the darkness. 5 God named the light "day" and the darkness "night." Evening gave way to morning. That was day one.

Amazing! It's happening again. The sun is starting to shine once more. The evening shadows of confusion and the dark fog of Satan's lies and deception are starting to melt away and dissipate. Once more my goals are becoming clear. My aim is much better. I can see the bulls-eye clearly now. HalleluJAH! Praise the Lord! Jesus is Lord! And the Light has come!

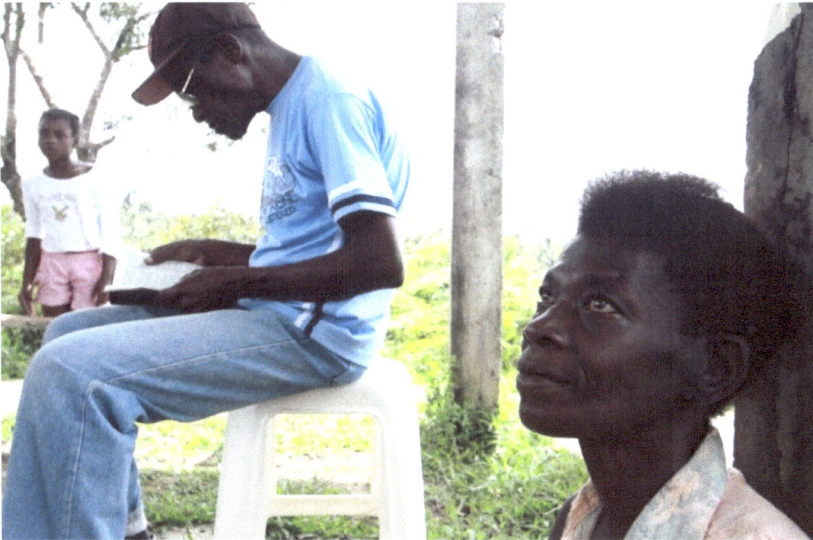

CLARITY

God had a plan and followed it through.

10. Full Circle: The Cycle is Complete the Perfection of Divine Order Re-established –

The number 10

This began as a quest I called "10 Days To Total Financial Freedom" ... why not 20 days or 40 days? Why 10? Good question. All I know is I had a desire to write 10 days and not some other number. In doing some research I discovered some interesting things about this number. Not everyone puts stock in the meaning of numbers in the Bible but some do and they have made some interesting discoveries. BibleStudy.org is one of the sites that has a lot of good study material on this and many other subjects.

In general the number 10 is one of the perfect numbers and signifies the perfection of Divine order. Completeness of order, marking the entire round of anything, is, therefore, the ever-present signification of the number ten. This implies that nothing is wanting; that the number and order are perfect; that the whole cycle is complete.

For Example:

Noah was the tenth generation from Adam - Noah completed the antediluvian age in the tenth generation from God creating man.

The Ten Commandments - The Ten Commandments contain all that is necessary, and no more than necessary, both as to their number and their order, while the Lord's prayer is complete in ten clauses.

The 10 clauses of the Lord's Prayer -

1. God's Sovereignty

2. God's manifest name

3. The realization of God's kingdom

4. First mentions the earth

5. The gift of grace supplying our need

6. Treatment of man's sin

7. Pleads for spiritual guidance

8. Pleads for final deliverance from all evil

9. Sums up the divine glory

10. Completes the eternal cycles

These are only a few of the many examples of the usage of the number 10 in the Bible.

The number 10 also often illustrates **the fullness of whatever is in view, without it necessarily being the totality.** For example

Ten Days to Total Financial Freedom

Monday would be a full day, but not the totality of the week. Likewise the number 10 in "10 Days To Total Financial Freedom." The 10 represents the fullness or the completion of this quest for financial freedom. This might not be a literal 10 days, but a period of time that brings a sense of fullness or completion to the project. It is bringing the perfection of Divine order into view so that nothing is wanting and the cycle is complete.

I believe the Holy Spirit inspired me to use this number for the purpose of this illustration and this project. When I began this search for financial freedom I had no idea where all of this would lead me. This was simply a 10 day goal I set for myself. As I write this it is now day 41 since I began this project. 40 days of prayer and serious seeking the Lord for the answers to one of life's most perplexing problems; poverty, lack, and want and in short, financial issues.

40 days. Not 10. It took me 40 days to reach this point where I felt it was time to speak out what God has spoken into me. 40 days to come to this place of fullness with the subject of finances in view; A 40 day cycle bringing the perfection of Divine order and a sense of completeness with nothing wanting.

My 10 days to achieving this goal is in reality a literal 40 days. But this is what the number 10 signifies, a bringing to completion, or, in this case, coming to a logical, Biblical conclusion, in a certain time frame regardless of how long or short it is. In other words, doing whatever it takes, for however long it takes, to achieve your desired goal. Resolving in your heart to pursue something you desire until the something becomes a reality. This is what I have done.

And now for the conclusion to the matter; by conclusion I mean fully understanding the material in view, but not exhausting the full revelation of the whole council of God on this subject. This is for the reader to pursue further at his or her own leisure and according to their own desires. I have been in hot pursuit of gaining God's wisdom and understanding concerning financial freedom for the past 40 days and a lifetime of Christian service before that. Now it's up to you to set a goal and pursue that goal with all your might until the answer comes.

God's Order – The Journey - Clarity

Let's now bring further clarity and complete this cycle of pursuit by studying the life of a young man named Joseph on his journey as he is separated from his father's house as a shepherd, sold as a slave into Potiphar's house in Egypt, falsely accused and placed in the house of bars as a prisoner, raised to prominence in Pharaoh's house as Prime Minister, and finally, after many years, restoration with his father and family, bringing everything full circle and completing the journey according to God's perfect plan and divine order.

As a young man, Joseph, the favored son of Jacob his father, also received significant dreams from the Lord which indicated that someday he would have a position of leadership and his family would bow to him as a result. The combination of his father favoring him and this interpretation of his dreams enraged his brothers. They began to plot how they could kill him or in some way get rid of him. This led to them catching him one day unawares, stripping him of his coat of many colors, given to him by his father in an act of favoritism, and then throwing him into a well. The wisdom of Reuben, Joseph's older brother prevailed and they decided not to kill him. Instead he was sold as a slave for twenty pieces of silver to some passing Ishmaelite traders who took him to Egypt. This was done in Rueben's absence. Rueben's plan was to rescue Joseph from the well and return him to his father later because his conscience bothered him greatly.

This is how the story goes ...

Genesis 37:30-36

New Living Translation (NLT)

30 Then he went back to his brothers and lamented, "The boy is gone! What will I do now?"

31 Then the brothers killed a young goat and dipped Joseph's robe in its blood. 32 They sent the beautiful robe to their father with this message: "Look at what we found. Doesn't this robe belong to your son?"

33 Their father recognized it immediately. "Yes," he said, "it is my son's robe. A wild animal must have eaten him. Joseph has clearly been torn to pieces!" 34 Then Jacob tore his clothes and dressed himself in burlap. He mourned deeply for his son for a long time. 35 His family all tried to comfort him, but he refused to be comforted. "I will go to my grave[a] mourning for my son," he would say, and then he would weep.

36 Meanwhile, the Midianite traders[b] arrived in Egypt, where they sold Joseph to Potiphar, an officer of Pharaoh, the king of Egypt. Potiphar was captain of the palace guard.

Joseph, the favored son of his father is now sold as a slave to Potiphar in Egypt. Talk about a sudden change of events and status. But the favored son of Jacob is also the favored son of God, his heavenly Father.

Genesis 39:1-6

New Living Translation (NLT)

Joseph in Potiphar's House

39 When Joseph was taken to Egypt by the Ishmaelite traders, he was purchased by Potiphar, an Egyptian officer. Potiphar was captain of the guard for Pharaoh, the king of Egypt.

2 The Lord was with Joseph, so he succeeded in everything he did as he served in the home of his Egyptian master. 3 Potiphar noticed this and realized that the Lord was with Joseph, giving him success in everything he did. 4 This pleased Potiphar, so he soon made Joseph his personal attendant. He put him in charge of his entire household and everything he owned. 5 From the day Joseph was put in charge of his master's household and property, the Lord began to bless Potiphar's household for Joseph's sake. All his household affairs ran smoothly, and his crops and livestock flourished. **6 So Potiphar gave Joseph complete administrative responsibility over everything he owned. With Joseph there, he didn't worry**

about a thing—except what kind of food to eat!

Joseph was a very handsome and well-built young man,

The blessing of the favored son continues. The blessing of the Lord follows him to Egypt and in spite of his social status as a slave he soon rises to the top and Potiphar places him in charge of his entire estate. What seemed like a demotion in the beginning turns into a great promotion. From a lowly shepherd boy earning no respect from his peers, in his earthly father's house, to well earned respect as chief administrator in the house of the captain of the guard for Pharaoh, the king of Egypt.

Hello? Are you still with me?

However, in Potiphar's house there is one problem. Potiphar's wife has a crush on this good looking Hebrew slave and she wants to have sex with him. Joseph resists this temptation.

8 But Joseph refused. "Look," he told her, "my master trusts me with everything in his entire household. 9 No one here has more authority than I do. He has held back nothing from me except you, because you are his wife. How could

I do such a wicked thing? It would be a great sin against God."

Joseph recognizes this would be a sin against God and refuses her offer, but Potiphar's wife is persistent and day after day she approaches him until finally one day in desperation Joseph run out of the house to escape. Potiphar's wife who had hold of his sleeve found herself holding his jacket when he tore away from her and fled. Realizing she was being shunned she shouted "rape!" Using his jacket as her proof she convinced everyone in the house including her husband that Joseph was guilty.

Joseph Put in Prison

19 Potiphar was furious when he heard his wife's story about how Joseph had treated her. 20 So he took Joseph and threw him into the prison where the king's prisoners were held, and there he remained. **21 But the Lord was with Joseph in the prison and showed him his faithful love. And the Lord made Joseph a favorite with the prison warden.** 22 Before long, the warden put Joseph in charge of all the other prisoners and over everything that happened in the prison. 23 The warden had no more worries, because Joseph took care of everything. **The Lord was with him and caused everything he did to succeed.**

So now we have Joseph the favored son of Jacob reduced to slave status and now to prisoner. We can see a steady downward progression. Yet there is one thing that remains constant no matter where he is socially or circumstantially. His status with God remains the same. So regardless of where he finds himself, whether as a shepherd, a slave in Egypt, or a prisoner, God's favor is upon his life and he soon finds favor with men and is rewarded with promotion. As with Potiphar, the prison warden soon discovered that with Joseph in charge everything increased, multiplied, and was successful. God's favor also wins the favor of man regardless of our circumstances.

In prison Joseph met the King of Egypt's chief butler and chief baker who had fallen from grace. One night they each had a dream which greatly troubled them. Noticing this, Joseph asked them what was the problem. They replied, "we both had dreams last night, but there is no one here to tell us what they mean." Joseph replied, "Interpreting dreams is God's business, tell me what you saw."

God's man with God's favor and God's wisdom interprets the dreams telling them that the butler would be restored to his job again as chief butler in three days. Joseph asked the butler to please mention him to Pharaoh upon his arrival back in the palace and ask the king to please have mercy upon him and have him released.

When the chief baker saw that the butler's dream had a good meaning he promptly told his. However his dream had a different meaning. "In three days Pharaoh will take off your head and have your body impaled on a pole and the birds will come and pick off your flesh."

Three days later both dreams came true as Joseph had said, however, the chief butler promptly forgot about Joseph's request, never giving him a thought. Genesis 40:23.

Two years later Pharaoh had two dreams one night. They greatly troubled him and he had no one to help him understand their meaning. None of the magicians or sages of Egypt could help him either. Finally the butler remembered his sin and told the story of how the young Hebrew slave had properly interpreted the dream of his and that of the baker while they were together in prison. Pharaoh sent at once for Joseph. After a quick shower, shave, and change of clothes, Joseph appeared before Pharaoh. The Pharaoh related the two dreams to Joseph. Once again God's man with God's favor and God's wisdom replies, "I can't do it by myself, but God will tell you what it means."

Genesis 41:17-46

The Voice (VOICE)

Pharaoh: 17 In my dream, I was standing on the bank of the Nile River, 18 and seven healthy, fat cows came up out of the Nile River and grazed in the grassy reeds at the river's edge. 19 Then seven other cows came up after them. They were miserable, very ugly and thin. Never had I seen such horrible-looking cows in all the land of Egypt. 20 Anyway, the thin, ugly cows ate the first seven fat cows. 21 But after they had eaten them, no one would have known they had done so because they were still as ugly as before. Then I woke up. 22 I fell asleep and dreamed a second time. I saw in this dream seven ears of grain, all plump and fine, growing on one stalk. 23 And then seven ears that were withered, shriveled up, and burnt by the east wind sprouted after them. 24 The thin ears swallowed up the seven good ears. When I told the magicians about these dreams, there was no one who could explain them to me.

Joseph (to Pharaoh): 25 Pharaoh's dreams are one and the same. God is revealing to Pharaoh what He is going to do. 26 The seven good cows are seven years and the seven good ears are the same seven years—years of plenty. Both dreams tell one story. 27 The seven thin and ugly cows that came up after them are also seven years, as are the seven thin ears burnt by the east wind.

These are seven years of famine. 28 As I told Pharaoh, God is showing Pharaoh what He means to do and what will come. 29 There will be seven years of great abundance throughout all the land of Egypt. 30 But after that, there will be seven years of famine. Whatever abundance was once enjoyed will be totally forgotten, because the famine will consume the land. 31 The famine will be so severe that no one will know what it is like to have enough of anything.

32 The doubling of Pharaoh's dream means this future is fixed by God, and He will make it happen very soon.

33 My advice is that Pharaoh should select someone who is wise and discerning and put him in charge of the land of Egypt during this time. 34 Pharaoh should appoint officers over the land and direct them to take one-fifth of all that the land of Egypt produces during the seven abundant years, 35 gather it together, store it up, and guard it under Pharaoh's authority. That way each city will have a supply of food. 36 The food would then be held in reserve for the people during the seven years of famine that are sure to come to Egypt. In this way, the people of Egypt will not starve to death during the famine.

37 Pharaoh and all his advisors liked Joseph's suggestion.

Pharaoh (to his advisors): 38 Is there anyone else you know like Joseph who has the Spirit of God within him?

39 (to Joseph) Since God has shown all of this to you, I can't imagine anyone wiser and more discerning than you. 40 Therefore you will be in charge of my household. All of my people will report to you and do as you say. Only I, because I sit on the throne, will be greater than you. 41 I hereby appoint you head over all of the land of Egypt.

42 As a symbol of his power, Pharaoh removed the signet ring from his hand and put it on Joseph's. Then he dressed him in fine linens and put a gold chain around his neck. 43 He had Joseph ride in the chariot reserved for his second-in-command, and servants ordered everyone, "Kneel!" as he rode by. So this was how Pharaoh appointed Joseph head over all of the land of Egypt. 44 But Pharaoh had one more declaration.

Pharaoh (to Joseph): I am Pharaoh, and I decree that no one may do anything in the land of Egypt without your consent.

45 Then Pharaoh gave Joseph an Egyptian name, Zaphenath-paneah, and arranged for him to marry an Egyptian woman, Asenath (daughter of Potiphera, priest of On). **So this was how**

Joseph gained authority over all the land of Egypt.

Pharaoh wants there to be no doubt that Joseph is his second-in-command. So he holds a formal ceremony and presents Joseph with special gifts, symbols of high office and power. He gives Joseph his signet ring, mounted with Pharaoh's personal seal. He dresses him in royal garb and provides him with the finest chariot available. He issues decrees that put Joseph in charge of all affairs in Egypt. Finally, to top it off and to make sure this son of Israel would be fully accepted into Egyptian society, he gives him an Egyptian name and arranges a marriage with a high-profile priestly family. Just a few hours before, Joseph was a prisoner. Now he is in charge of all the land.

46 Now Joseph was 30 years old when he entered into Pharaoh's service. He left the king of Egypt's presence to travel throughout the land.

Now is this an amazing account of God's grace or what?

From favored son as shepherd in the house of Jacob

To favored slave as administrator in the house of Potiphar

To favored prisoner as administrator in the house of bars

To favored administrative statesman in the house of Pharaoh.

My Lord! And in and through all of this Joseph was never in debt, never had an unpaid bill, never wondered about where his next rent payment would come from. He never had an overdue mortgage payment. He never had an overdue credit card. He never had a late camel payment. All his transportation costs from one place to another were covered. All his housing costs were supplied . And in all of this, his journey from prisoner to Prime Minister happened in a single moment of time.

GOD'S FAVOR!!!

There's more to this story which I encourage you to read. But for our purpose we will end it here.

God's favor! It all began when he was a teenager looking after his father's sheep. But even before this he had favor with his dad. And this favor was not because of Joseph's goodness or his unique abilities. It was simply because he was the son of Jacob's old age and he favored him because of this.

In Joseph's journey from shepherding his father's flock as a young boy to shepherding the people of Egypt there is one thing that runs as a common thread. GOD'S FAVOR. This favor was not earned it was given. It was a gift. Joseph did not ask for this favor from either his earthly father or his Heavenly Father. It is the gift of God. It is this favor that sustained him and increased him wherever he went. God's favor was his security, his unlimited source of supply. God's favor never failed him. He never experienced an economic crisis. He never encountered a housing shortage. His table was always full. Joseph was blessed with an unlimited supply of supernatural abundance. The favor of God supplied his every need and promoted him at every level; the favor of God seen him safely through every storm he encountered and prospered him and exalted him. Joseph was blessed because of the goodness of God not because of his own goodness. It was the gift of God.

Now we have come full circle. In the beginning God said, "Let there be light: and there was light" So now we will end where we began; walking in the light of God's Word and His truth which sets us free from the bondage of misplaced trust and twisted thinking. We are at this place where the darkness collides with the light and the light prevails, as always. We are at this place where the two ways meet, Gods way and my way. We are at this place where we drop anchor out there where the water is deeper. And we cast our nets of self-doubt, self-interest, self-seeking, and self-exaltation overboard into the water of God's Promise, and there, we will "see what we will catch." We put up the "white flag" and we surrender completely and finally to the wisdom and the will of God. We sow the seed "not my will be done" into the rich soil of "His will be done." And surely in this place of dying to self there will be a rich harvest; an overflowing harvest; an abundant harvest. The "catch" will be great as well as humbling.

As Joseph was honored and favored by someone much greater than himself, so are we. God loves us, not because of our goodness, but because of His goodness. God is love, therefore He loves. Jacob loved the son born to him in his old age. God the Father loves us in similar fashion. God loves us because we are His creation, the sheep of His pasture. We are highly favored of God and He has also provided a coat of many colors for us who receive Him by faith. It is a coat of Salvation, a coat of Righteousness, a robe of Sanctification and Holiness, a garment of Grace and Truth, a robe of Praise, of Peace, of Joy, which God's own Son gives to us freely when we come to Him in humble faith and obedience confessing Him as Lord and Savior and welcoming Him into our lives. He robes us and crowns us with His love, His peace, His joy. He seals us and calls us His own with the kiss of favor from the Holy Spirit, the down payment of our eternal inheritance.

The favor of God; this is what Joseph carried with him wherever he went and the favor of God never failed him or let him down. Joseph made sure that this account with God was always topped up and that his relationship with Him was always right. Remember Potiphar's wife? Joseph placed his relationship with God ahead of any other, no matter how enticing and tempting. His account with God was always full. Joseph never concerned himself about his bank account or where his next meal would come from as long as he maintained his relationship with his Father in heaven and kept a balanced account there. Joseph's security was not in things he possessed. It was in his relationship to God, not earthly wealth.

Favor with God. This is the place of total financial freedom. This is the place I need to aim for. How long will this take? It depends. How determined am I to do things God's way? How stubborn is my will in surrendering to faith in the promises of God? How convinced am I that God's Word is truth and cannot lie? What value do I place on this relationship with Joseph's

God? What has more value for me?; a large bank account?; or a large promise from God? Where is my trust? In things I can see, touch, smell? Or is it focused on the Invisible Triune God, "Father, Son, Holy Spirit," and His eternal Word? What's more important? The favor of God?; or the favor of man and created things?

FAVOR! FAVOR! FAVOR! GOD'S FAVOR! How important is God's favor to me? What value do I place on this relationship with Him? What value do I place on God's favor? If my name is Abraham my answer is , "no price is too great to live in the favor of God." If my name is Joseph my answer is, "from the pit to the Palace, from prison to Praise, from prisoner to Prime Minister, from obscurity to Prominence, from the earthly to the Heavenly, from bowing to others to others bowing to me, from an insignificant shepherd boy despised by my peers to shepherding the flock of Egypt, wearing the King's own signet ring, robed in beautiful clothing, the royal gold chain around my neck, in charge of all the land of Egypt, the chariot of the second-in-command, and honored by everyone, everywhere I go!" If that's not enough I was also given a new name meaning "he has the godlike power of life and death!" On top of this I was given a wife. I am thirty years old. I was 17 when I left my father's fields and started on this journey which has led me to this place.

And That's Not All

And that's not all. Remember the dreams when I was a young boy? They have all come to pass now just as I was shown. My family is all here with me now. Reunited, once again I have seen my father. I have been rejoined with my family here in Egypt where God brought me by His Divine hand of favor and blessing so I could save the lives of many people." (Genesis 50:19-21).

The favor of God? You're asking me about the favor of God? What would I trade for it? Nothing! What value do I place on God's favor? Reread the words of my testimony you just read ... then read them again ... and again ... and again ... until ... they sink down ... deep down ... deep in the rich soil of your heart and soul. Let this revelation of the favor of God take root there. Water this garden often with the word of God, the promises of God. Let a marriage take place. As the seed falling into the earth marries the rich soil through its death and becomes one with it, so allow your will to fall into the rich soil of "God's will be done in your life." There in this place of total surrender to the will and the heart of God you will discover great treasure, great wealth, great abundance, an astonishing harvest. You will discover the richness and the vastness of the favor of God out there where the water is a "little deeper." Out there a little bit farther into this pool of God's favor you will drop your nets and you will "see what you will catch." Out there I see the Light of a new beginning reflecting off a "white Flag" of full surrender to the Master's voice.

God: 3 **Let there be light.**

And light flashed into being. 4 God saw that the light was beautiful and good, and He separated the light from the darkness. 5 God named the light "day" and the darkness "night." Evening gave way to morning. **That was day one.**

This is day one. This is the beginning. The place we start.

We have now come full circle. 10 Days To Total Financial Freedom is more about a journey than about a destination or a time frame. It is more about a lifestyle than about an event. It is more about the size of my faith in the Person and the Promises of God then it is about the size of my bank account or my income. It is more about God than about money. It is more about the eternal than about the temporal. It is more about me and my relationship with God than it is about me and money. It is more about caring and sharing than about receiving and reaping. It is more about sowing and growing than looking for gain. It is more about setting my eyes upon the promises of God than about setting my eyes upon monetary value. It is more about seeking the favor of God and balancing my account with him than it is about seeking man's favor. It's more about carrying the favor of God than carrying a bank card. It's more about a heart full of faith and trust in God's promise than a bank account full of money. It's more about having a Favor Account with God than a money account with the local banker.

It's about coming into the Light of God's truth and the security of His favor. It's about me opening a new account with the Master of the Universe and maintaining my relationship with Him. It's about knowing Him who promises to never leave me nor forsake me. It's about walking and living in the promises of God and enjoying the benefits of His favor. It's about making Joseph's God my God. It's about abiding in the True Vine, Jesus Christ, the New Testament Joseph, Highly Favored Son of the Father (Matthew 3:16-17, Mark 9:1-8, John 3:33-36), and following Him no matter what.

Isaiah 45:1-3

The Voice (VOICE)

45 This is what the Eternal One says to His chosen agent, Cyrus the Persian.

God has a special mission for Cyrus, the Persian emperor: to lead the world and free His exiled people. The Scripture is clear: God, not kings, directs history. Kings—and sometimes their subjects—often need to be reminded of that. The Eternal, the one True God, stands above and behind human history, directing and orchestrating its events.

Eternal One: Not by his hand alone, but with his in Mine, nations are vanquished, their leaders conquered; Doors and gates open without a fight and will not close.

2 (to Cyrus) I will go ahead of you and smooth the way, lower the heights, break down bronze doors, and cut through iron bars.

3 I will give you hidden treasures and wealth tucked away in secret places; I will reveal them to you. Then you will know that I am the Eternal, the God of Israel, who calls you by name.

The Spirit of God has called you and I by name as surely as He called Cyrus generations ago, and for the same purpose, to set the captives free, and bring reconciliation with the Father through Christ the Son.

The Spirit of God says to us, *"**Deep in the heart of the Father you will find your treasure. Not hid from you, but hid there for you to discover.**"*

This day is day one. Now the rest is up to you.

God bless you

Marvin

About the Author

As a born again Christian for more than 30 years and a serious student of God's Word I believe I have a valid claim to speak His Word on this subject of finance according to the Bible.

Ten Days to Total Financial Freedom

My faith in God and His calling on my life has led me to many countries, as a friend to the poor and hurting, involved in various projects. From delivering humanitarian aid and Bible's in the Russian language, to spiritually starved Ukrainians after the fall of Communism and the former Soviet Union, to supporting orphanages in India, to helping 85,000 poverty stricken Soviet Union Jews make "Aliyah" to Israel.

In addition, at the Lord's command, and with His help, the help of my family, and many others, I re-opened, and re-established an old country church which had been abandoned for 10 years prior. I've had my share of poverty, living and ministering to the poor in under privileged areas. And I am absolutely convinced God has a better plan. This plan, for man's blessing and increase, is contained in His Word. God's roadmap for success. I am all for helping the poor and needy, but I am also convinced that God also has a better plan for increase than continual handouts.

This plan is contained in the Word of God. "For I know the thoughts I think towards you, saith the Lord, thoughts of peace, and not of evil, to give you an expected end." Jeremiah 29:11 KJV. In other words, God's plan for the poor, the destitute, and those struggling to survive financially, is to give them a hope and a future.

Praise God! That's what this book and my life is all about. Discovering the plan of God for my own life and helping others find God's better plan for theirs. I am married and presently living in Colombia, South America, where I am ministering to … you guessed it … the poor. I'm telling everyone about the goodness of God and that His plan for their lives is a good one, for increase and multiplication, and not an evil plan for more suffering, defeat, and misery. This is the power of the Word of God to set the captives free! Amen!

Your friend for multiplication, increase, and God's very best in your life.

Marvin Swanson

www.toallnations.net

Serving Communion/The Lord's Table to parents, adults, and all who will come in the "Church Without Walls" in a remote jungle village near the Pacific west coast of Colombia. (Soldiers camping nearby overnight used the wood from the walls for firewood, thus, no walls). "Suffer not the little children to come unto Me," Jesus said. Matthew 19:14 (even the dogs are patiently looking for a crumb to fall to the ground so they can join us in our devotion). More than 100 were served, with lunch and donated Christmas gifts following. There were a lot of happy people. Praise God! December 2012.

Ten Days to Total Financial Freedom

Contact Information

Author: Marvin Swanson
Address: Canada/Colombia
Email: acts29missions@yahoo.com

: mascanada1947@gmail.com

Phone: 780 747 9051
Facebook: Marvin Swanson
Twitter:@SwansonMarvin

Other titles also available on Amazon:

One Flock One Shepherd

Mary Martha Principle

Whatever He Says To You, Do It

Romans 10:8-13

New King James Version (NKJV)

[8] But what does it say? "The word is near you, in your mouth and in your heart"[a] (that is, the word of faith which we preach): [9] that if you confess with your mouth the Lord Jesus and believe in your heart that God has raised Him from the dead, you will be saved. [10] For with the heart one believes unto righteousness, and with the mouth confession is made unto salvation. [11] For the Scripture says, "Whoever believes on Him will not be put to shame."[b] [12] For there is no distinction between Jew and Greek, for the same Lord over all is rich to all who call upon Him. [13] For "whoever calls on the name of the LORD shall be saved."[c]